The Unofficial HEATED RIVALRY COOKBOOK

Quarto.com

First Published in 2027 by The Harvard Common Press, an imprint of The Quarto Group,
100 Cummings Center, Suite 265-D, Beverly, MA 01915, USA.
T (978) 282-9590 F (978) 283-2742

EEA Representation, WTS Tax d.o.o.,
Žanova ulica 3, 4000 Kranj, Slovenia.
www.wts-tax.si

The Harvard Common Press titles are also available at discount for retail, wholesale, promotional, and bulk purchase. For details, contact the Special Sales Manager by email at specialsales@quarto.com or by mail at The Quarto Group, Attn: Special Sales Manager, 100 Cummings Center, Suite 265-D, Beverly, MA 01915, USA.

31 30 29 28 27   1 2 3 4 5

ISBN: 979-8-3179-0270-4

Digital edition published in 2027

Library of Congress Control Number: 2026944788

Cover Design: Tanya Jacobson, tanyajacobson.co
Design: Cindy Samargia Laun
Illustration: Kate Francis
Cover Image: Kate Francis

Printed in Guangdong, China TT082026

The Unofficial HEATED RIVALRY COOKBOOK

Recipes Inspired by Love, Hockey, and Food

MICHELLE ANDERSON | CHRIS PETERSON

HARVARD COMMON PRESS

ILLUSTRATIONS BY KATE FRANCIS

04

HOME TEAM DINNERS 72

05

DRINKS WORTHY OF *THE* CUP 104

06

DESSERTS TO CHEAT FOR 126

FOOD.
HOCKEY.
LOVE.

INTRODUCTION

Food. Hockey. Love. At first glance, it's easy to think they don't have much in common (especially if you're not a hockey fan). But the truth is, they all share an incredibly important part of life: passion. It doesn't matter whether you're trying to score a hat trick on the ice, creating your own masterpiece meal to impress that special someone (or a whole room of them), or just flirting to communicate your true feelings to that new-found crush. Passion makes all the difference.

That steamiest of emotions is actually a big key to the runaway success of the hit TV show *Heated Rivalry*, and the Game Changers book series by Rachel Reid that spawned the small-screen fan favorite. Sharp-edged competition and magnetic, sparkly chemistry make the characters and story lines beyond fascinating. But it is the love and passion—of Ilya and Shane, Scott and Kip, and all the others—that bring the stories to vivid life and have so deeply touched the hearts of readers and viewers alike.

After all, who wouldn't be moved by Scott Hunter's heart-wrenching self-imposed isolation, his overwhelming fear of letting anyone in on his secret, of breaking down the walls he had worked so hard to construct? Until he meets Kip.

You're made of stone if you aren't profoundly moved by the moment Scott kisses Kip, consummating their relationship on center ice for all the world to see. He celebrates his greatest professional victory with the greatest prize any of us could ever hope for—true love. It's a remarkably brave and fearless moment But then, that's the power of love and passion. They can make us leap tall buildings in a single bound.

So . . . Food. Hockey. Love. They excite us. They are born of passion and fuel the passion that makes life so much more interesting, more fun, and more wonderful.

Maybe you've never shouted through the glass as your team's star center powers the puck into the net, but surely you've known the pulse-quickening thrill of new love? That first kiss and flush of fever you feel across the back of your neck. The tingling when that special someone gently, casually, almost accidentally links fingers with you as you walk side by side?

On the same note, you've no doubt eaten a dish that delights your tongue and thrills your senses. Something that transcends mere food or sustenance. We all have our favorite foods, and they offer so much more than simple nutrition. They make us happy. They can be an antidote to a bad day, or a salve over the wounds from a fight with that favorite person. The right food at that right moment comforts us, triggers fond memories, and adds sunshine to a rainy day. It helps us remember the good times and get through the bad.

The fact is, food is woven in with all our other passions, including hockey and love. The condiment-slathered hot dog or cheese-draped nachos a fan might scarf down watching Montreal, Boston, or New York play defines that night's victory with immensely satisfying flavors. The snacks make the moment more fun. They become part of a cherished memory.

And who ever forgets the first meal they make from scratch for their new love? It really doesn't matter if that repast is a humble tuna melt or carefully crafted shrimp scampi; the flavors, aromas, and the meal itself forever become a part of the romantic experience and happy recollections. The story of your relationship will, in the future, be told around that meal. Such is the magnificent power of food.

If we're being honest, we know that every instance of passion is about the perfect bit of heat, the exact right mix of spices, and . . . the ideal mouth feel. (Interpret that as you will . . .)

That said, passion isn't everything. The flame that burns hottest can easily burn itself out. There is also a time and a place for simple, loving companionship. For modest sustenance and meals that don't necessarily make a statement. For the calm repetition of practice in preparation for competition. Everyday stuff, but rich nonetheless.

The stories of *Heated Rivalry*, and the Game Changers series as a whole, are about passion, but also about much more than burning desire. They capture the hearty lust of love and the scalding fire of competition, but the simple bump of Shane and Ilya's shoes under a table speaks just as loudly about their bond as a violent body check into the boards does. The simple, steady backing of Kip's and Shane's parents, and Scott's teammates, says volumes about the elegant beauty that lies in the gifts of tolerance, loving support, and acceptance. After all, there's room under the sun for all of us and there is a reason why a rainbow is woven of so many different colors.

This book and every recipe in it are a celebration of all that.

A Flavor for Every Taste

We all know that Scott has his Kip, and Shane and Ilya have each other. But Ryan also has Fabian. Eric has Kyle. And Troy has his Harris. We love who we love, and our hunger wants what it wants.

That's why the recipes in this book were selected to create a wonderful tapestry of foods, flavors, and dishes. There is something for every preference and a solution to any particular craving you might have. (Well, any culinary craving!) Many of these hint at the books or television show. The blueberry smoothie on page 111, for instance.

Others, though, are simply inspired by the many *Heated Rivalry* characters and circumstances we have come to adore. It might be the moment a championship is won and Shane gets to exultantly hoist the cup overhead for the first time. Or it could be when Kip first gathers with his gang at the bar for beers, bar snacks, and a night of watching his boyfriend on TV. Or it could be inspired by hometowns, best friends, or off-the-ice excursions (including the cottage). There are lots of people, places, and occasions to memorialize in food, and that's the goal of the recipes in each chapter.

As with the characters themselves, diversity is key. Sometimes we crave the sweetness of Harris giving Troy the grace to heal (with a spoonful of cookie dough ice cream). Other times, we want the saltiness of the Boston locker room at the moment Ilya's captain speech reaches its profane crescendo. Whatever flavor you're after, you'll find it somewhere in these recipes.

Many of these are the height of simplicity and easy to whip up. Others are a bit more challenging, requiring time and focus. But let's be clear; all of these creations are totally achievable for even the novice cook. They are in your wheelhouse. If Shane can follow a recipe, so can you. Regardless of the relative complexity and the unique combination of ingredients, each recipe in its own way captures the passion, the fire, and the excellence that defines *Heated Rivalry*.

In fact, these recipes are a little like the hockey players and characters in the series. One may be elegant or decadent, while another is kind of plain and workaday. That doesn't change the fact that all are endearing and charming in the right setting.

Want a hearty breakfast for the morning after that first steamy night? Look no further than the fundamental goodness and joy of homemade waffles with raspberry syrup (page 35). Looking to impress a new heartthrob with an upscale homemade meal? We've got you covered with a first-date and Valentine's Day dinner.

Every course and every occasion are covered. There are meals to start your day off with a bang and get you out the door raring to go. There are meals that you can bring to your better half in bed as a loving gesture, to spark the leisurely morning cuddling to come. Some are simple meals meant to evidence big feelings, like the tuna melt on page 47 that Ilya made for Shane or the burgers Shane made for him in return (page 49).

You'll find easy-peasy snacks to satisfy guests at a rollicking watch party on your second (or tenth) reheat, or to just hold you and a friend over from lunch to dinner. There is a collection of drinks to slake any thirst and a selection of tantalizing desserts that put the exclamation point on any meal. Those will leave a lovely sweetness lingering on the tongue, much as the right kiss lingers on the lips.

Heated Rivalry teaches us many things, including that, sometimes, you have to wait for the love of your life (which is, by the way, totally worth the wait). But you should never have to wait for a meal you'll love and love to share . . . and now you don't have to.

THE DOUBLE MEANINGS OF HOCKEY LINGO

Backcheck:
1) Skating backward toward your own goal to disrupt the other team's offense
2) Ogling that buff someone's butt

Bar Down:
1) A precise shot on goal that deflects off the top cross bar into the net
2) Your favorite night spot closed due to family emergency

Beauty:
1) A talented teammate who is a great locker-room presence
2) A hunky teammate who is a great locker-room presence (*rowrrr*)

Body Check:
1) A hit on an opposing player to stop them from controlling the puck
2) Purposely-on-accident bumping into that hunky guy at the bar

Breakaway:
1) A fast-skate move leaving the player with the puck unopposed to the goal
2) Getting the hunk's number that everyone else wanted

Celly:
1) Unbridled, pure joy celebration with teammates right after scoring a goal
2) Congratulatory outburst from a circle of friends after you reveal a new love

Chirp:
1) Trash talk
2) Flirty trash talk

Cross Checking:
1) An illegal move in which a player uses the stick handle to block an opponent
2) Surreptitiously looking at your partner's text messages

Dangle:
1) Slang for a hockey stick
2) A certain man part

Five Hole:
1) The scoring point between the goalie's legs
2) 'Nuff said

Grinder:
1) High-energy, relentless teammate who presses a physical game up and down the ice
2) A physically passionate and exuberant romantic partner

Hand Pass:

1) Knocking the puck to a teammate using your mitt
2) A lingering brush of the fingertips across just about any part of your crush's body

Hip Check:

1) Hip-forward, low-center-of-gravity bump of a player to interrupt his progress
2) Intimate hip-to-hip bump on the dance floor

Hooking:

1) Using the stick blade to tangle up an opposing player
2) Um . . . a practice that involves pay for play?

Icing:

1) Slapping the puck from behind the red line to cross the opposing goal line without another player touching it
2) Not responding to texts or emails

Pinch:

1) Risky play whereby a player on defense tries to hold the blue line and clear the zone when an opposing player has the puck
2) A risky play whereby a player shows affection by plucking the target's tuchus

Sauce:

1) A skill pass lifting the puck off the ice, over an opponent's stick, and precisely to a teammate
2) The moisture one leaves behind after nibbling a beloved's neck

Shootout:

1) A tie-breaker competition involving one-on-one penalty shots alternating between teams
2) Two friends flirting with the same hunk

Sieve:

1) A goalkeeper who allows a lot of goals
2) Your bestie who can't keep a secret about the person you're crushing on

Snipe:

1) A hard, super accurate shot on goal that hits where it's hardest for the goalkeeper to reach
2) Zeroing in one's flirtations on a single target in the bar

Twig:

1) Slang for the hockey stick
2) An unimpressive appendage

01

GOLD-MEDAL BREAKFASTS

Hockey superstars need fuel in the tank if they're going to perform at an elite level. Problem is, cooking and eating a full breakfast can be a bit of a challenge when you're facing a 5 a.m. ice time. That's why they tend to lean toward super-healthy, calorie- and nutrient-dense smoothies like the ones in chapter 5.

But the rest of us mere mortals? We usually get up at a more reasonable hour and have the luxury of cooking and enjoying a robust, tasty, and filling start to the day. That's where the recipes in this chapter come in.

They say that breakfast is the most important meal of the day because it sets the tone and gives you the raw calories you'll need to tackle whatever's coming in the hours that follow. But why would you choose not to start your day in the most delicious way possible? (Spoiler alert: That way is not a cold toaster pastry wolfed down in the car on the way to work.)

The good news about the powerhouse recipes in this chapter is that they were developed with the *Heated Rivalry* couples in mind. Although eating a leisurely breakfast is ideal, all of these recipes acknowledge that time spent together is precious for Ryan and Fabian, Harris and Troy, and the rest of the guys. They want to share filling, tasty breakfasts without wasting too much of that together time fussing in the kitchen.

That's why even the most indulgent of these recipes is meant to come together simply and relatively quickly. Some even accommodate the busy schedule we know so well from the on-season training Ryan, Ilya, Scott, and all hockey players have to endure. For instance, the Champion's Grab-and-Go Breakfast Burrito on page 15 is a tastebud-delighting full meal in a handy-dandy portable package. You can even make it the night before!

Of course, certain delectable options—like the Ricotta Pancakes with Strawberry Compote on page 19—are designed to be savored. They beg to be shared and eaten more slowly, sitting at the table with a favorite person or even a whole bunch of favorite people. When you have the time, a big part of enjoying life means meandering through a leisurely breakfast like one you might enjoy during the summer in a certain lakeside cottage.

Champion's Grab-and-Go
Breakfast Burrito

The pace in New York moves a little more quickly than it might in Ottawa. So, if you're a big-city dweller like Scott Hunter, it's handy to have a few breakfast options that you can eat on the move. That's where this tasty, filling, portable hunger-crusher comes in. It rolls up a healthy dose of protein, high-nutrition veggies, and a modest number of carbs. **Serves 2**

1 tablespoon (15 ml) olive oil
½ small sweet onion, diced
2 teaspoons minced garlic
1 pound (454 g) ground turkey (93% lean)
1 teaspoon chili powder
1 teaspoon ground cumin
½ teaspoon sea salt
¼ teaspoon freshly ground black pepper
2 tablespoons (33 g) tomato paste
2 (12-inch, or 30 cm) flour tortillas
1½ cups (168 g) shredded aged cheddar cheese
1 large ripe avocado, sliced or mashed
¼ cup (65 g) diced tomato
2 tablespoons (12 g) chopped scallion, green parts only
1 tablespoon (14 g) unsalted butter

Bulk up your burritos by dividing ½ cup (65 g) cooked basmati rice and ¼ cup (65 g) drained black beans between them.

1. In a large skillet over medium-high heat, heat the olive oil. Add the onion and sauté for 3 to 4 minutes, or until softened. Stir in the garlic and sauté for 30 seconds.
2. Add the ground turkey and cook, breaking it up until it's browned, about 8 minutes. Stir in the chili powder, cumin, salt, and pepper. Cook until fragrant.
3. Add the tomato paste and cook for 2 minutes, until the mixture is rich and slightly saucy. Remove from heat, cover, and set aside.
4. In a large dry skillet over medium heat, warm the tortillas. (Or microwave for about 20 seconds.) Keep covered with a clean kitchen cloth while you work to keep them soft and pliable.
5. Lay each tortilla flat. Layer fillings down the center in this order: cheese, turkey filling, avocado, tomatoes, scallions, and extra cheese. Fold in the sides and roll tightly from the bottom to seal.
6. In a large skillet over medium heat, melt the butter. Place each burrito seam-side down. Toast for 2 to 3 minutes per side, or until they are golden brown and the cheese is fully melted.
7. Serve hot, or wrap cooled burritos tightly in foil and refrigerate up to 3 days. Reheat in a 350°F (177°C) oven or air-fryer until heated through.

Easy Weekend Blinis

When he first moved from Moscow to Boston, Ilya Rozanov would have brought his favorite sneakers, his mother's necklace, a burning desire to win, and not much else. But perhaps he also carried an aching hunger for the Russian version of pancakes. Make a batch of these, especially topped with the classic *smetana* (Russian sour cream) and caviar, and you'll see for yourself. **Makes 24 to 38 blinis**

1 cup (240 ml) whole milk, heated to between 105°F (41°C) and 115°F (46°C)

2¼ teaspoons active dry yeast

1 teaspoon granulated sugar

¾ cup (100 g) all-purpose flour

½ cup (74 g) buckwheat flour

½ teaspoon sea salt

2 large eggs, separated

1 cup (227 g), plus 3 tablespoons (45 g) sour cream or *smetana*, divided

2 tablespoons (28 g) unsalted butter, melted, plus more for greasing

4 ounces (113 g) salmon roe

Chopped fresh dill

Lemon wedges

1. In a small bowl, combine the warm milk, yeast, and sugar. Let stand for 5 to 10 minutes, or until foamy.
2. In a large bowl, whisk together the flours and salt. Make a divot in the center. Pour in the yeast mixture, egg yolks, 3 tablespoons (45 g) sour cream, and butter. Whisk until smooth.
3. Cover the bowl with a clean kitchen cloth and set aside in a warm place for 45 to 60 minutes, until slightly puffed up.
4. In a medium bowl, beat the egg whites to soft peaks using a hand mixer. Gently fold the whites into the risen dough.
5. Preheat the oven to 250°F (120°C).
6. Grease a large skillet with butter over medium-low heat. Working in batches, drop tablespoon portions of batter onto the skillet.
7. Cook each blini for 1 to 2 minutes, or until bubbles form. Flip and cook for 1 minute more. Repeat until the batter is used up, keeping the blinis warm in the oven.
8. To serve, top each blini with a dollop of sour cream and a small scoop of salmon roe. Finish with chopped dill and a squeeze of lemon.
9. Store cooled blinis in the refrigerator for up to 2 days. Rewarm in a skillet over medium-low heat, or in a warm oven.

25¢
SUGAR, SUGAR
BOYS DON'T CRY
IT'S RAINING MEN
SUGAR SHACK
I WILL SURVIVE
PINK PONY CLUB
BORN THIS WAY
TOM'S DINER
ALICE'S RESTAURANT
ESPRESSO
I'M COMING OUT
SUGAR MAGNOLIA
POUR SOME SUGAR
SAME LOVE

Ricotta Pancakes
with Strawberry Compote

A native Vermonter takes his pancakes very, very seriously. So, even if Eric doesn't quite realize the relevance of the moment Kyle brings him to a diner for the quintessential Green Mountain State breakfast, it's monumental. There was no better way to work up an appetite than a chilly hike full of stunning vistas and more than a few longing thoughts, and no better way for Kyle to put his heart—so carefully guarded and protected—on the plate for Eric. **Serves 4**

FOR THE COMPOTE

2 cups (340 g) strawberries, hulled and halved

3 tablespoons (45 ml) pure maple syrup

1 tablespoon (15 ml) lemon juice

FOR THE PANCAKES

1 cup (248 g) ricotta

¾ cup (180 ml) buttermilk, room temperature

3 large eggs, room temperature

2 tablespoons (28 g) unsalted butter, melted, plus more for the pan

1 teaspoon pure vanilla extract

1 teaspoon lemon zest

1 cup (120 g) all-purpose flour

2 tablespoons (25 g) granulated sugar

1 teaspoon baking powder

½ teaspoon sea salt

Pure maple syrup

MAKE THE COMPTE

1. In a medium saucepan over medium heat, combine the strawberries, maple syrup, and lemon juice. Cook until softened, stirring frequently, 6 to 8 minutes.
2. Crush the berries with a potato masher. Set aside or transfer to a resealable container and refrigerate for up to 1 week. (Warm before serving.)

MAKE THE PANCAKES

1. In a large bowl, whisk the ricotta, buttermilk, eggs, butter, vanilla, and lemon zest until well blended.
2. In a small bowl, whisk together the flour, sugar, baking powder, and salt. Fold into the ricotta mixture.
3. Heat a large skillet over medium heat and add a small amount of butter. Working in batches, scoop four ¼-cup (60 ml) batter portions into the skillet.
4. Cook until bubbles form on the surface of the pancakes, 2 to 3 minutes. Flip and cook until both sides are golden and there is no wet batter in the middle, about 2 minutes. Repeat with the remaining batter.
5. Serve three pancakes per person topped with maple syrup and a generous dollop of strawberry compote. Refrigerate cooked pancakes up to 3 days. Reheat in toaster or oven until warmed through.

Moscow Morning Kasha
with Caramelized Onions and Mushrooms

There are many reasons why Moscow is no longer "home" for Ilya Rozanov. The evil brother. The dead parents. The oppressive authorities. But, most especially, the brutal weather. Moscow winters are a whole different definition of cold, beyond anything Boston or Ottawa can dish out. Buckwheat kasha is the Russian answer to dealing with extreme low temperatures in the tastiest way possible. **Serves 4**

1 cup (180 g) toasted buckwheat groats

2 cups (474 ml) chicken or vegetable stock

5 tablespoons (70 g) unsalted butter, divided

1 teaspoon sea salt, divided

Freshly ground black pepper

2 large sweet onions, sliced thin

12 ounces (340 g) mixed mushrooms (cremini, shiitake, and oyster), sliced

2 teaspoons minced garlic

If desired, top each dish with chopped fresh dill, crème fraîche or sour cream, and a soft-boiled egg.

1. Rinse the groats under cold water and drain well.
2. In a large saucepan over medium-high heat, bring the stock, 2 tablespoons (28 g) butter, and ½ teaspoon salt to a boil. Add the groats, cover, and reduce the heat to low. Simmer for 18 to 20 minutes, or until tender.
3. Remove the saucepan from the heat and let rest for 10 minutes, covered. Fluff with a fork and season with pepper.
4. Meanwhile, melt the remaining butter in a large skillet over medium-low heat. Add the onions and ½ teaspoon salt and sauté for 10 to 12 minutes, or until softened.
5. Reduce the heat to low and sauté for 25 to 35 minutes, stirring occasionally, until the onions are deep amber and jammy. Push them to one side of the skillet.
6. Increase the heat to medium-high and add mushrooms. Sauté until the moisture evaporates and mushrooms brown, about 10 minutes. Stir in the garlic and sauté 1 minute more. Season lightly with pepper.
7. Fold the onion-mushroom mixture into the kasha, or spoon kasha onto plates and top, as preferred. Refrigerate leftover kasha for up to 4 days. Reheat with a splash of stock or water to restore the texture.

Montreal's Best Eggs Benedict

Throughout the books and TV series, we see Yuna as a caring and supportive "momager." If she had a favorite meal, it would probably be brunch, as it conveniently falls after those early-morning hockey practices. Born in Montreal, her absolute fave brunch would probably be the city's hometown version of eggs Benedict. She and the other hockey moms would certainly enjoy this dish while brunching and comparing notes on their young superstars. **Serves 4**

3 large egg yolks
1 tablespoon (15 ml) lemon juice
½ cup (113 g) unsalted butter, melted
Pinch cayenne pepper
Sea salt
1 teaspoon Dijon mustard, optional
8 slices thick-cut Canadian bacon
1½ tablespoons (21 ml) white vinegar
8 large eggs
2 tablespoons (28 g) salted butter
4 English muffins, split and toasted

The sauce can be made in a blender. Blend the yolks, lemon juice, salt, cayenne, and mustard, if using, for seconds. With the motor running, slowly stream in the melted butter, 25 to 30 seconds. Go slow and steady, and don't be intimidated!

1. In a medium heatproof bowl set over a pot of gently simmering water, combine the egg yolks and lemon juice. Whisk until thickened and pale, about 3 minutes.
2. Slowly drizzle in the butter while whisking constantly. Whisk until the sauce is thick, smooth, and glossy. (If the sauce thickens too much, whisk in 1 teaspoon warm water.)
3. Season with the cayenne and salt to taste. Stir in the mustard, if using. Keep the sauce warm (on or near the warm stove, but off the heat) while preparing the rest of the ingredients.
4. Heat a large skillet over medium heat and cook the bacon for 2 to 3 minutes per side, or until crispy at the edges. Remove from the skillet and keep warm.
5. While the bacon is cooking, bring a shallow saucepan of water to a simmer over medium heat. Reduce to low so it is barely simmering, and add the vinegar.
6. Crack an egg into a small bowl. Stir water in the pan to create a whirlpool, and then slide egg into water; depending on the size of your saucepan, you can poach more than 1 egg at a time. Cook for 2½ to 3 minutes, or until the white is set and yolk remains soft. Remove the egg with a slotted spoon and drain on paper towel. Repeat with all the eggs.
7. Lightly butter each toasted muffin half and put two on each plate. Top each with a slice of bacon and a poached egg. Spoon hollandaise generously over top and serve immediately.

The Morning-After Omelet

This is not the wake-up-and-wash-away-the-regret recovery breakfast. (*That* breakfast is the French toast on page 31.) No, this is for those more pleasant, luxurious morning-afters that follow the first torrid night before. Like when Kyle first stays over at Eric's killer brownstone, for instance, and Eric serves him a perfect omelet. This meal is simple, satisfying, fulfilling, and filling. Kind of like the night before. **Serves 1**

3 large eggs

Sea salt

Freshly ground black pepper

½ tablespoon unsalted butter

2 tablespoons (14 g) grated Gruyère or sharp cheddar

1 tablespoon (3 g) chopped fresh chives

1 large ripe heirloom or vine tomato, sliced

1 teaspoon extra-virgin olive oil

Dash balsamic vinegar, optional

2 slices artisanal bread (sourdough, brioche, or country loaf), toasted

Salted butter, softened

1. In a medium bowl, combine the eggs with a pinch of salt and pepper. Whisk until emulsified and lightly frothy.
2. Heat an 8-inch (20 cm) nonstick skillet over medium-low heat for 1 to 2 minutes, just to warm but not hot. Add the unsalted butter and swirl until foamy, but not browned.
3. Pour in the eggs and gently stir in small circles with a spatula while shaking the pan. Continue stirring until small soft curds form but the surface remains wet, about 3 minutes.
4. Smooth the eggs into an even layer and reduce the heat to low. Sprinkle the cheese and chives down the center.
5. Use a spatula to fold a side over the filling, then gently roll the omelet over into the classic shape. Cook for 30 to 45 seconds more, or until just set. Slide the omelet onto one half of a plate.
6. Line the tomato slices beside the omelet. Drizzle them with olive oil and lightly season with salt and pepper. Drizzle with the balsamic vinegar, if using.
7. Spread each slice of toast with the salted butter, stack the slices beside the omelet, and serve.

05:15AM

Overnight Oats
for Early Ice Time

Balance is important, in hockey, food, and life. To every Ilya, there should be a Shane. The brute-force crunch of a Ryan is balanced by the elegant smoothness of a Fabian. The jaded saltiness of a Troy creates a dynamic tension with the natural sweetness of a Harris. Similarly, this simple, delightful meal in a jar captures that balance: It's creamy and crunchy, tangy and sweet. Bonus: It's basically a delicious, no-cook, set-it-and-forget-it nutritional powerhouse that can be wolfed down in a minute on your way to an early morning practice (or whatever you have going on). **Serves 4**

1½ cups (340 g) plain Greek yogurt

1 cup (240 ml) unsweetened almond milk or preferred milk, plus more as needed

3 tablespoons (30 g) chia seeds

2 to 3 tablespoons (30 to 45 ml) pure maple syrup or honey

1 teaspoon pure vanilla extract

½ teaspoon ground cinnamon

Pinch sea salt

2 cups (192 g) old-fashioned rolled oats

1 cup (200 g) diced fresh strawberries

1 cup (200 g) diced ripe mango

2 tablespoons (10 g) toasted coconut flakes, optional

2 tablespoons (15 g) chopped pistachios, optional

1. In a large bowl, whisk together the yogurt, milk, chia seeds, maple syrup, vanilla, cinnamon, and salt until smooth.
2. Stir in the oats until evenly coated. Gently fold in the strawberries and mango, reserving a little for garnish if desired. (For firmer texture, add the fruit just before serving instead.)
3. Transfer the mixture to 4 lidded, individual serving jars (like jelly jars or mini-Mason jars) or a single resealable container. Refrigerate for at least 6 hours, or up to overnight, until thick.
4. Stir to loosen and add a splash of milk if needed. Top with any reserved fruit and sprinkle with toasted coconut and nuts, if using. Serve cold.

New York–Style Bagel
and Lox

You don't have to play for the Admirals to appreciate a proper New York everything bagel and lox. It's the sort of thing Scott Hunter probably takes for granted living in the city, but New York put it on the map. Dress your own and you'll enjoy the purely tongue-pleasing explosion of salty, sweet, tangy, creamy, crunchy, and luxurious. For such a modest nosh, it packs huge flavors and textures! **Serves 4**

8 ounces (226 g) full-fat cream cheese, softened
1 tablespoon (15 ml) lemon juice
1 teaspoon lemon zest
2 tablespoons (4 g) minced red onion
1 tablespoon (15 g) diced capers
1 tablespoon (3 g) minced fresh dill
Freshly ground black pepper
4 everything bagels, split
8 to 10 ounces (227 to 283 g) lox
1 large ripe avocado, sliced
Lemon wedges
Fresh dill sprigs

Slice the avocado just before serving to avoid browning.

1. In a medium bowl, combine the cream cheese, lemon juice, zest, onion, capers, and dill. Use a hand mixer to whip until smooth and lightly aerated. Season with pepper and chill for 10 minutes to firm slightly for spreading.
2. Toast the bagel halves. Spread a generous layer of lemon cream cheese on each half.
3. Drape folded ribbons of lox over the cream cheese. Top with avocado slices and a sprinkle of pepper.
4. Serve open-faced on a board or plate with lemon wedges and dill. The cream cheese can be refrigerated for up to 1 week.

Hangover French Toast

Sometimes you have to drop your guard, let loose, and see what wild adventures the night holds. Maybe you head out to Montreal's hottest hangouts. Perhaps you're a little less fancy and you just want to throw back some beers at Kip's favorite New York haunt. Either way, make it to last call and the morning comes far too soon. That's when a comfort-food breakfast comes in handy. The cure it delivers is like a hug that makes everything all better. **Serves 4 to 6**

Unsalted butter for greasing

8 thick-cut, day-old slices artisanal sourdough

6 large eggs

1 cup (240 ml) heavy whipping cream

¾ cup (180 ml) whole milk

3 tablespoons (45 ml) bourbon

2 tablespoons (30 ml) pure maple syrup, plus more for serving

¼ cup (53 g) packed light brown sugar

2 teaspoons pure vanilla extract

1½ teaspoons ground cinnamon

¼ teaspoon kosher salt

12 slices thick-cut bacon

For a bit of crunch, before baking, top with a mixture of ⅓ cup (71 g) packed light brown sugar, 3 tablespoons (24 g) all-purpose flour, ½ teaspoon ground cinnamon, and a pinch of salt, with 3 tablespoons (42 g) cold, cubed unsalted butter cut in.

1. Butter a 9 x 13-inch (23 x 33-cm) baking dish. Shingle the bread slices in a single layer.
2. In a medium bowl, whisk the eggs until completely blended. Whisk in everything else but the bacon.
3. Pour the custard slowly over bread in the baking dish, pressing down gently to saturate the slices. Cover the dish and refrigerate for at least 2 hours, but preferably overnight.
4. Preheat the oven to 350°F (175°C). Remove the baking dish from the refrigerator 20 minutes before baking.
5. Bake uncovered for 40 to 45 minutes, or until the custard is set and the top of the toast is caramelized. Remove and let the toast rest for 10 minutes before serving.
6. Meanwhile, arrange the bacon in a large skillet and set over medium heat. Cook, flipping, until crispy on both sides, 12 to 14 minutes. Drain on paper towels.
7. Slice French toast into thick slabs and transfer to plates, spooning warm custard over the top. Serve with maple syrup and bacon on the side. Refrigerate leftover French toast for up to 3 days; reheat in a 325°F (165°C) oven.

Hard Body Muffin-Cup Egg Bites

Shane (and his teammates, for that matter) doesn't just accidentally have the type of stacked-blocks abs that peg a hotness meter into the red. And he doesn't get there by loading up on carbs or sugars. Nope. He maintains his eye-candy-ness by scarfing muscle-building protein and performance-fueling healthy fats. That's exactly what you find in these tasty little breakfast snacks that pack an enforcer's punch.

Makes 12 bites

1 tablespoon (15 ml) olive oil, plus more for greasing

10 ounces (283 g) lean ground turkey

2 teaspoons minced garlic

½ teaspoon smoked paprika

10 large eggs

1 cup (184 g) liquid egg whites

¾ cup (170 g) full-fat cottage cheese

½ teaspoon Dijon mustard

½ teaspoon sea salt

¼ teaspoon freshly ground black pepper

1 cup (112 g) shredded aged sharp cheddar

¼ cup (36 g) diced red bell pepper

2 tablespoons (4 g) minced sweet onion

¼ cup (14 g) chopped baby spinach

1. Preheat the oven to 325°F (165°C). Generously grease a 12-cup muffin tin or use silicone liners.
2. In a large skillet over medium heat, heat the olive oil until it's shimmering. Add the turkey, garlic, and paprika. Break the turkey up into fine crumbles as it browns, 6 to 8 minutes. Remove from heat and set aside.
3. In a blender, combine the eggs, egg whites, cottage cheese, mustard, salt, and pepper. Blend on medium for 20 to 30 seconds, or until smooth and lightly frothy. Stir in (don't blend) the cheddar.
4. Divide the turkey mixture evenly among the muffin cups. Top with the bell pepper, onion, and spinach. Fill each cup three-quarters full of the egg custard. Use a fork to evenly distribute the ingredients.
5. Bake for 22 to 28 minutes, or until the center of each cup is just set. Cool on a wire rack for 5 to 10 minutes before removing the cups and serving. Refrigerate for up to 3 days in a sealed container.

Love's Wonder Waffles

Fabian Salah's music career was on the upswing before Ryan Price came back into his life, but he wasn't entirely what you'd call "financially successful." He was, though, rich in friends. Their Sunday brunch tradition proved that a little culinary creativity, a cozy table filled with good food and drink, and some gossip is all anyone needs to put a lousy week behind them. Is it any wonder, then, that Ryan saw love in the simplicity of great waffles, coffee, and Fabian? **Makes 6 to 8 waffles**

FOR THE SYRUP

2 cups fresh (150 g) raspberries

½ cup (99 g) granulated sugar

1 tablespoon (15 ml) lemon juice

FOR THE WAFFLES

2 cups (240 g) all-purpose flour

2 tablespoons (25 g) granulated sugar

1 tablespoon (8 g) baking powder

½ teaspoon sea salt

2 large eggs, separated

1¾ cups (397 g) buttermilk, room temperature

½ cup (120 ml) whole milk, room temperature

½ cup (113 g) unsalted butter, melted and cooled slightly, plus more for greasing

1 tablespoon (15 ml) pure vanilla extract

FOR THE WHIPPED CREAM

1 cup (240 ml) heavy whipping cream, cold

2 tablespoons (16 g) confectioners' sugar

1 teaspoon pure vanilla extract

2 tablespoons (28 g) mascarpone

MAKE THE SYRUP

1. In a medium saucepan over medium heat, combine the ingredients. Bring to a gentle simmer for about 8 minutes, stirring and crushing the berries.
2. Strain the syrup for a smooth texture, or leave it unstrained for a more rustic style. Keep warm.

MAKE THE WAFFLES

1. Preheat the oven to 200°F (95°C). Preheat a waffle iron on medium-high.
2. In a large bowl, whisk together the dry ingredients.
3. In a small bowl, whisk together the egg yolks, buttermilk, milk, butter, and vanilla. Pour into the dry ingredients and mix until just combined.
4. In a medium bowl, beat the egg whites with a hand mixer to medium-stiff peaks. Gently fold the whites into the batter in two stages, keeping as much air as possible.
5. Lightly grease the waffle iron. Working in batches, use ¾ to 1 cup (180 ml to 240 ml) batter per waffle and cook until deep golden brown and crisp, 4 to 6 minutes. (Follow manufacturer's instructions.)
6. Keep waffles warm in the oven until ready to serve.

MAKE THE WHIPPED CREAM

1. In a medium bowl with a hand mixer, beat the heavy cream, confectioners' sugar, and vanilla to soft peaks. Add the mascarpone and beat until firm.
2. Serve waffles topped with a spoonful of warm raspberry syrup and a dollop of whipped cream. Refrigerate left-overs and reheat waffles in a toaster.

02

SHARED SECRETS, SANDWICHES & SALADS

Sandwiches and salads are like the rare, all-purpose utility players on the ice, those standouts that can handle just about any position reasonably well. All the offerings in this chapter can easily serve as an informal lunch, a simple and filling dinner, or an in-between snack when hunger gets the best of you.

The more wonderful thing about these particular recipes, though, is their adaptability. It's easy to put your own spin on things, like Kip did when he made Scott a chicken salad *without* feta, or like Ilya does when he cooks the first meal he'll share with Shane when Shane visits him in Boston. Hard to get things wrong when there is so much to go right.

That adaptability also means substitutions are easy. Not a fan of the pistachios in the First Valentine's Salad on page 41? No worries. Trade them out for some pecans or pine nuts, or do without the nuts entirely. Your crush will still enjoy the heck out of that healthy expression of love on a plate. Or maybe you'd like to use the unusual Bro Buterbrød on page 53 as the centerpiece for your lunch with your own special "brø," but brown bread is not your jam (funny enough, it goes great with jam!)? Fear not. It's just as unique with rye or pumpernickel.

These are all easily scalable, as well. That means you can bump up the recipe from intimate lunch to a big old gathering with the whole team without missing a beat. (It also means you can scale them down if you're looking for a more intimate setting . . . and you can do the math.) Do it your way and make it your own.

It can be so easy to dismiss a sandwich or a salad as a simple thing, but certain versions come to have big meaning in the *Heated Rivalry* universe, which makes them worth a try in anybody's book.

Off-the-Ice Summer Pasta Salad

If you're going to skate hard and hit harder, like Ryan Price, you can't be eating gut bombs that weigh you down. So even though this is a perfect "summer" salad and ideal when paired with something like the Steak-a-Bobs for Sharing on page 77, it's also a healthy choice for hockey enforcers and office types alike. The pasta here is cooked al dente, but it's no secret that lots of people like their pasta (and their men) a little on the softer side—as Ryan does Fabian. **Serves 6 to 8**

1 pound (454 g) fusilli pasta

⅓ cup (80 ml) extra-virgin olive oil, plus more for pasta

1 cup (113 g) trimmed and cut green beans

1 cup (150 g) cherry tomato halves

1 cup (124 g) diced zucchini

1 cup (124 g) diced yellow squash

1 red bell pepper, seeded and diced

½ cup (71 g) diced red onion

½ cup (73 g) sliced sugar snap peas (on the bias)

½ cup (150 g) halved Kalamata olives

3 tablespoons (45 ml) lemon juice

2 teaspoons Dijon mustard

1 small clove garlic, minced

½ teaspoon sea salt, plus more for pasta water

¼ teaspoon freshly ground black pepper

½ cup (10 g) thinly sliced fresh basil

¾ cup (84 g) crumbled feta

1. Bring a large pot of heavily salted water to a boil over high heat. Cook the pasta to al dente, following the package directions, about 12 minutes. Drain and rinse briefly under cool water to stop cooking.
2. Transfer the pasta to a large bowl and toss lightly with a drizzle of olive oil. Let cool to room temperature.
3. Add the vegetables to the cooled pasta. Toss until evenly coated.
4. Make the dressing: In a small bowl, combine the olive oil, lemon juice, mustard, garlic, salt, and pepper. Whisk until fully emulsified.
5. Drizzle the vinaigrette over the salad. Toss until evenly coated. Fold in the basil, and scatter the feta over the top.
6. Cover and refrigerate for at least 1 hour to a low the flavors to meld. Toss again before serving and season as needed.

First Valentine's Salad

Until he met Kip, Scott Hunter was likely an order-in, delivery kind of guy. But as we saw in *Game Changer*, the first Valentine's Day with his resident smoothie maker/historian (his first Valentine's Day *ever*) inspired the hockey superstar to grab his apron and craft a special meal, starting with a simple but satisfying salad. Follow his lead for a light and delicious first course that leaves plenty of room for what's to come. **Serves 4 to 6**

3 tablespoons (45 g) Dijon mustard

2 tablespoons (30 ml) champagne vinegar

1 teaspoon honey or maple syrup

1 small clove garlic, minced

½ teaspoon sea salt

¼ teaspoon freshly ground black pepper

½ cup (120 ml) extra-virgin olive oil

6 cups (255 g) fresh baby spinach or spring mix, washed and dried

½ small red onion, thinly sliced, optional

1½ cups (225 g) small strawberries, hulled and halved

½ cup (56 g) crumbled goat cheese

⅓ cup (40 g) shelled roasted pistachios

1. In a small bowl, whisk together the mustard, vinegar, honey or syrup, garlic, salt, and pepper. Slowly drizzle in the olive oil while whisking constantly, until the dressing is thickened and fully blended. Taste and adjust the seasoning as needed.
2. In a large salad bowl, toss the salad greens and onion, if using. Season lightly with salt and pepper.
3. Drizzle half of the vinaigrette over the salad. Toss until evenly coated. Add more dressing as needed. The leaves should be just coated, not dripping.
4. Sprinkle with the strawberries, cheese, and nuts. Gently toss, then serve. Extra vinaigrette will keep refrigerated up to 1 week.

Penthouse Room-Service Caesar Salad

If you're keeping a relationship on the down-low, it's wise to eat in. That doesn't mean you have to eat badly, as this easy-to-make salad proves. The salad hinges on a distinctively salty, anchovy-forward dressing and the addition of flavor-rich salmon, perfectly suited to the dressing. And while the dressing is certainly delicious, if Shane and Ilya's passion taught us anything, it's that so is the undressing. **Serves 4**

¾ cup (180 ml) extra-virgin olive oil, divided, plus more for pan

3 tablespoons (45 ml) lemon juice, divided

1½ teaspoons minced garlic

Sea salt

Freshly ground black pepper

4 (5 to 6 ounce, or 142 g to 170 g) skinless salmon fillets

2 anchovy fillets, mashed (or substitute 1 teaspoon anchovy paste)

2 tablespoons (24 g) mayonnaise

2 cloves garlic, minced to paste

2 teaspoons Dijon mustard

1 teaspoon Worcestershire sauce

½ cup (40 g) grated Parmigiano-Reggiano

1 teaspoon garlic powder

3 cups (168 g) 1-inch (2.5 cm) chunks day-old sourdough or rustic bread

2 large heads romaine lettuce, chopped or hand-torn

¼ cup (28 g) shaved Parmigiano-Reggiano, plus more to serve

Lemon wedges

1. In a shallow baking or casserole dish, whisk together 2 tablespoons (30 ml) olive oil, 1 tablespoon (15 ml) lemon juice, minced garlic, and a pinch of salt and pepper. Dredge the salmon to coat evenly and lay it in the dish. Cover and refrigerate.
2. In a medium bowl, whisk together the anchovies, mayonnaise, garlic paste, mustard, 2 tablespoons (30 ml) lemon juice, and Worcestershire sauce until smooth.
3. Slowly drizzle in ½ cup (120 ml) olive oil while whisking constantly until emulsified. Stir in the grated cheese. Taste, and season as needed. Refrigerate.
4. Preheat the oven to 375°F (190°C). Line a baking sheet with parchment paper.
5. In a medium bowl, combine 2 tablespoons (30 ml) olive oil, garlic powder, and some salt and pepper. Add the bread and toss until completely coated. Spread out on the baking sheet.
6. Bake for 12 to 15 minutes, turning once, until golden brown and crisp. Set aside to cool.
7. Heat a drizzle of olive oil in a large skillet over medium-high heat. Place the salmon, top-down, in the skillet. Sear on each side for 3 to 5 minutes, or until it takes on color and is just cooked through but still moist inside. Transfer to a plate to rest for 3 minutes.
8. In a large, chilled salad bowl, toss the romaine with half the dressing until evenly coated. Add the croutons and shaved cheese and toss again. Add more dressing as needed.
9. Divide the salad among 4 plates. Top each with a salmon fillet, and sprinkle with additional shaved cheese and pepper. Serve with lemon wedges.

Chicken Salad
for Contenders

While lounging in the apartment, Kip tells Scott that he made him a pasta salad with chicken but no feta, indicating a deeper knowledge about Scott's tastes (at least in the kitchen). Flip the script by making this filling chicken salad that has no pasta. Either way, the sentiment is the same: You make food for those you love (the contenders for your heart) as a gesture of affection. Oh yeah, and also because you're jonesing for a champion-level chicken salad like the best New York delis make. **Serves 6**

½ cup (113 g) light mayonnaise
¼ cup (57 g) plain Greek yogurt
1 tablespoon (30 g) Dijon mustard
1 tablespoon (15 ml) apple cider vinegar
1 tablespoon (15 ml) lemon juice
1 tablespoon (21 g) honey
1 tablespoon (8 g) poppy seeds
½ teaspoon sea salt, or to taste
¼ teaspoon white pepper, or to taste
4 cups (480 g) diced or shredded cooked chicken
1 large Granny Smith apple, julienned, tossed with lemon juice
½ cup (76 g) halved seedless red grapes
⅓ cup (33 g) finely sliced celery
¼ cup (26 g) chopped pecans
2 tablespoons (15 g) minced red onion
Freshly ground black pepper

1. In a medium bowl, whisk together the mayonnaise and yogurt until smooth. Add the mustard, vinegar, lemon juice, and honey. Whisk until emulsified.
2. Stir in the poppy seeds. Season to taste with the salt and white pepper.
3. In a large bowl, toss together the chicken, apple, grapes, celery, pecans, and onion until mixed. Drizzle with the dressing and gently toss until the salad is completely coated. Cover and refrigerate for at least 1 hour before serving.
4. Dust with black pepper and serve cold. Refrigerate leftover salad, covered, for up to 3 days.

GINGER ALE

Lovers' Tuna Melt

Food often says what we find hard to voice. Ilya Rozanov isn't one to gush, or even do much more than tease or clown around. That's why it's such a big deal when Ilya makes Shane this simple sandwich the first time Shane visits Ilya's home. Food is a language of love and the importance of what was being said—and that it was said at all—is not lost on either person. **Serves 4**

2 (5-ounce [113 g]) cans white albacore tuna, packed in water, well drained

⅓ cup (76 g) mayonnaise

1½ tablespoons (22 ml) lemon juice

2 tablespoons (15 g) minced celery

2 tablespoons (15 g) minced red onion

¼ teaspoon sea salt

¼ teaspoon freshly ground black pepper

1 large French baguette, sliced on the bias into 8 (½-inch-thick [12 mm]) slices

2 tablespoons (28 g) unsalted butter, softened

1½ cups (168 g) shredded sharp white cheddar

Potato chips, to serve, optional

1. Flake the tuna into a medium bowl, separating some larger chunks for texture. Fold in the mayonnaise and lemon juice until just combined.
2. Stir in the celery and onion. Taste, and season with salt and pepper. Refrigerate for 10 to 15 minutes to allow the flavors to marry.
3. Preheat the oven to 400°F (200°C)
4. Arrange the bread on a baking sheet. Spread each slice with the butter. Toast for 3 to 5 minutes, or until light golden brown but still tender inside.
5. Spoon a generous mound of tuna salad onto each bread slice and spread it to the edges. Top with cheese.
6. Return to the oven for 3 to 4 minutes, or until the cheese is melted, bubbling, and lightly blistered. (Rotate the pan once.) Transfer to plates and serve hot with chips on the side, if desired.

Cozy Cottage Smash Burgers

As one of the cutest cooking moments ever, it went from page to screen nearly unchanged. Shane shows off his grill skills during Ilya's visit to his cottage by whipping up a couple burgers—plus six more—because the recipe made eight. Ilya's deadpan observation, that a person with any sort of math skills could just cut the recipe in half, became an instant classic. Ah, you gotta love Shane. As Ilya does, and everyone at your cottage will, when you make the appropriate number of these juicy, flavor-filled burgers. **Serves 8**

1 cup (226 g) mayonnaise
3 tablespoons (45 ml) ketchup
2 tablespoons (30 g) sweet pickle relish
1 teaspoon apple cider vinegar
2 teaspoons freshly ground black pepper, divided
3 tablespoons (42 g) unsalted butter, plus more for the buns
3 large sweet onions, thinly sliced
2 teaspoons sea salt, divided
3½ pounds (1.6 kg) ground chuck (80% lean)
Canola oil for grill
16 slices aged sharp cheddar
8 brioche buns
2 cups (40 g) shredded iceberg lettuce
2 large beefsteak tomatoes, sliced
8 dill pickle spears, sliced lengthwise

1. In a medium bowl, whisk together the mayonnaise, ketchup, relish, vinegar, and ½ teaspoon pepper until smooth. Cover and refrigerate for at least 30 minutes.
2. In a large skillet over medium-low heat, melt the butter. Add the sliced onions and ½ teaspoon salt. Cook for 15 minutes, or until softened.
3. Reduce the heat to low and cook for 20 to 25 minutes more, or until the onions are deep golden brown and jammy. Set aside.
4. Divide the beef into 16 portions and roll into balls. Flatten into burgers and sprinkle each with the remaining salt and pepper. Refrigerate, covered, until ready to cook.
5. Preheat the grill over medium-high, and grease the grates with canola oil. When the oil begins to smoke, you're ready to grill.
6. Cook the burgers, undisturbed, until they come off the grates without sticking, about 5 minutes. (Do not press down on the burgers.)
7. Flip, then grill according to the desired doneness: about 6 minutes for medium-rare (internal temp of 135°F or 57°C); about 7 minutes for medium (135°F or 63°C), or 8 minutes or more for well (150°F+ or 66°C+). Top each burger with cheese during the last 2 minutes of cooking and close the grill lid to melt. Let the cooked burgers rest while you prep the buns.
8. Butter the buns, if desired, before spreading with the sauce. Top the bottom halves with lettuce, two burgers, the cooked onions, tomatoes, and pickles. Close with the top halves, pressing down lightly, and serve warm.

19

Grind(him) Grinder

Here's a sandwich that goes down awfully easy. A nice sausage and some meatballs provide all the protein you could want, and the tasty sauce makes the eating easy. Hockey-star boyfriends enjoy a huge hero every now and again, and why not? It's perfectly filling and ideal for sharing. This is purely for the meat-eaters in the crowd. So, the question is: What hunger are you looking to satisfy? **Serves 4**

FOR THE MEAT

½ cup (66 g) Italian bread crumbs

⅓ cup (80 ml) whole milk

¾ pound (340 g) ground beef (80% lean)

½ pound (227 g) ground pork

¼ cup (20 g) grated Parmigiano-Reggiano

1 large egg

2 cloves garlic, minced

2 tablespoons (12 g) Italian seasoning

½ teaspoon sea salt

⅓ teaspoon freshly ground black pepper

3½ tablespoons (52 ml) olive oil, divided

¾ pound (340 g) sweet Italian sausages

1 small onion, diced

1 jar (24 to 32 ounces, or 680 to 907 g) good-quality tomato sauce with basil

FOR THE SANDWICHES

4 Italian sub rolls or hoagie buns

1½ tablespoons (21 g) unsalted butter, softened

1½ cups (168 g) shredded whole-milk mozzarella

½ cup (56 g) provolone, shredded

1. In a small bowl, combine the bread crumbs and milk. Set aside for 5 minutes.
2. In a large bowl, combine the beef, pork, soaked bread crumbs, cheese, egg, garlic, seasoning, salt, and pepper. Mix gently until just combined. Do not overwork.
3. Form into 12 to 14 golf ball–size meatballs.
4. In a large skillet over medium heat, heat 1 tablespoon (15 ml) olive oil. Sear the meatballs all over until browned. Transfer to a plate and set aside.
5. Add 1 tablespoon (15 ml) olive oil to the skillet. Add the sausages and sear all over, until browned and almost cooked through. Slice into 3-inch (8 cm) pieces and set aside.
6. Preheat the oven to 400°F (200°C). In a Dutch oven over medium heat, heat the remaining oil. Add the onion and cook for 5 to 7 minutes, or until soft. Add the tomato sauce. Bring to a gentle simmer. Add the meatballs and sausage. Cover and simmer, stirring occasionally, for 30 minutes, or until the sausage is fully cooked.
7. Split the sub rolls, leaving a hinge along one side, and spread with butter. Toast the rolls on a baking sheet for 5 to 7 minutes, or until crisp but still soft inside.
8. Coat inside of each roll with the tomato sauce. Arrange about 3 meatballs and 3 sausage pieces in each roll. Spoon extra sauce over the top of the meat, and sprinkle with the cheeses.
9. Return to the oven and bake 6 to 8 minutes, or until the cheese is melted and bubbling. Serve hot. Refrigerate leftovers for up to 4 days.

Bro Buterbrød

Homesickness means missing the flavors of home, as well as home itself. That's why hockey imports from Scandinavia, Germany, and Russia—even stars like Montreal's Sorren Miitka and New York's Matti Jalo—crave a taste of home when they're settling into a new country and a new team. This classic open-faced sandwich gives them that taste of home, one that is full of creamy, salty, crunchy satisfaction. Luckily, you don't need to be homesick to enjoy it! **Serves 4**

¾ cup (170 g) mayonnaise

2 cloves garlic, minced

1 teaspoon lemon juice

Sea salt

Pinch white pepper

1 tablespoon (3 g) minced fresh dill, plus more for garnish

1 large English cucumber, thinly sliced

4 thick slices brown bread (or rye, pumpernickel, or black bread)

2 tablespoons (28 g) unsalted butter, softened

2 tins (8.47 ounces, or 240 g) smoked sprats (*brisling*, or Nordic sardines), drained (or substitute 8 thin slices Black Forest ham)

Freshly ground black pepper

Lemon wedges, for garnish

1. In a small bowl, stir together the mayonnaise, garlic, lemon juice, salt, and white pepper until combined. Stir in the minced dill. Cover and refrigerate for at least 15 minutes (and up to 3 days).
2. Place the cucumber slices in a medium bowl and sprinkle with salt. Toss gently and let sit for 7 minutes. Drain and set aside.
3. Spread each bread slice with a thin layer of softened butter and then a generous layer of the garlic mayonnaise.
4. Arrange sprats (or ham) on each slice, and layer cucumber slices over. Season with black pepper and garnish with fresh dill. Serve open-faced on a platter or wooden board, with lemon wedges and extra garlic mayonnaise on the side.

03

GOT GAME, SNACKS & SIDES

It isn't just the heroes on the ice who work up an appetite during hockey games. All those unsung boosters in the seats put in a fair amount of effort. The vitally important work of berating the refs at full volume after bad calls, mercilessly taunting opposing players, and screaming wildly for one's home team can't be done on an empty stomach. You have to fuel that machine to keep it running.

That's why hearty snacks are part of any fan's game-day kit. Whether you're laying out a spread on the table while you warm up that wall-mounted monster TV, or you're shopping the concession level and munching in the stands at the rink, fandom is hungry work that requires tasty, filling grub. And that is the noble goal to which this chapter is dedicated.

These alluring options are, by their nature, a little decadent and maybe not the healthiest parts of anyone's diet. A palate-pleaser like Classic Canuck Poutine (page 57) isn't going to be part of any workout diet plan, and especially not if you're sculpting a finely tuned, eye-candy machine like Shane, Scott, or Ilya's hard bodies.

But even they would be the first to agree that sometimes . . . you satisfy the tongue first.

These dishes certainly do that, and they can do it on non-game days. They are good supporting players to the lunch or dinner team on the table. A tasty favorite like the bar fries on page 61 goes with sandwiches, soups, or mains at a cookout. So, enjoy these wherever your hunger takes you and consider them just part of the home-team crowd.

Classic Canuck Poutine

The maple-leaf nation has contributed a lot more to the world than most people realize. We have Canada to thank for insulin, IMAX, Shane Hollander, and the goalie mask that gave all those *Halloween* movies their signature vibe. Poutine may put all those contributions to shame, whether Troy Barrett likes it or not. He's lucky he has Harris for a lot of reasons, but especially to edit out his disparaging comments on this cheese-and-gravy–drenched pile of fries, shielding him from the ire of Ottawa fans. **Serves 4**

4 large russet potatoes (about 2½ pounds [1.13 kg])

1 tablespoon (15 ml) white vinegar

¼ cup (57 g) unsalted butter

¼ cup (30 g) all-purpose flour

2½ cups (593 ml) beef stock

1 tablespoon (17 g) tomato paste

1 teaspoon Worcestershire sauce

¼ teaspoon freshly ground black pepper

Sea salt

4 to 6 cups (948 ml to 1.4 L) vegetable oil

3 cups (336 g) white cheddar cheese curds, room temperature

Malt vinegar, optional

1. Peel the potatoes (or leave unpeeled if preferred) and cut into ½-inch (12 mm) thick fries.
2. Fill a large bowl with cold water and swish in the white vinegar. Soak the fries for 30 minutes. Drain, rinse well, and pat dry with paper towels.
3. Meanwhile, in a large saucepan over medium heat, melt the butter. Whisk in the flour to form a roux. Cook for 3 to 4 minutes, or until lightly browned with a nutty fragrance.
4. Slowly whisk in the beef stock until incorporated. Add the tomato paste, Worcestershire sauce, and pepper. Simmer for 8 to 10 minutes, whisking occasionally, until thick and glossy, but still pourable. Taste, and add salt as needed. Keep warm.
5. In a large, heavy pot or Dutch oven, heat the oil to 325°F (163°C). Set a wire rack over a tray or a paper towel–lined baking sheet.
6. Fry the potatoes in batches, for 4 to 5 minutes each, or until pale and tender. Don't allow the fries to brown. Transfer to prepared tray. Let the fries rest for at least 10 minutes.
7. Increase the oil temperature to 375°F (190°C). Fry the potatoes again for 2 to 3 minutes, or until deep golden brown and crisp. Remove and season immediately with salt.
8. Arrange the fries on a serving platter or in individual bowls. Scatter cheese curds generously over the fries. Ladle the gravy evenly over the top, allowing the curds to soften and melt slightly, and serve with malt vinegar, if desired. Refrigerate leftover gravy in a sealed container for up to 5 days.

Airport Lounge Trail Mix

Plane travel is a brutal part of life as a hockey pro. The game schedule may take you across the country and back—and even internationally if you play for your country in the International Ice Hockey Federation (IIHF) World Championship or the Olympics. Finding healthy, tasty snack food that doesn't cost half your contract is a challenge. The answer is to make your own. Even Shane's best friend, Hayden Pike, could make a batch of this while still watching the kids (well, most of them, anyway). **Serves 4 to 6**

2½ cups (148 g) Rice Chex cereal
1½ cups (46 g) Corn Chex cereal
1 cup (120 g) mini pretzel twists
½ cup (71 g) roasted almonds
½ cup (57 g) roasted cashews
½ cup (57 g) pecan halves
¼ cup (57 g) unsalted butter, melted
2 teaspoons Worcestershire sauce
½ teaspoon garlic powder
½ teaspoon onion powder
¼ teaspoon smoked paprika
¼ teaspoon dried mustard powder
¼ teaspoon freshly ground black pepper
¼ teaspoon seasoned salt
½ cup (57 g) dried cranberries

1. Preheat the oven to 275°F (135°C). Line 2 baking sheets with parchment paper.
2. In a large bowl, combine the cereals, pretzels, and nuts. Toss gently until thoroughly mixed.
3. In a small bowl, whisk together the butter, Worcestershire sauce, and spices.
4. Drizzle the wet ingredients over the dry. Toss until evenly coated. Spread out evenly on the baking sheets.
5. Bake for 35 minutes, stirring every 10 minutes, until toasted and aromatic. Remove and cool completely on the sheets.
6. Transfer the mix to a large bowl and stir in the cranberries. Serve, or store in a sealed container at room temperature up to 2 weeks.

Ultimate Bar Fries

The *Heated Rivalry* TV series weaves through many bars (and, not coincidentally, many drunken nights). So, it's no surprise that Shane meets his most famous beard, the lovely Rose Landry, in a bar where she's feasting on a plate of fries. She can't stop eating them. That's how you know great bar fries when you eat them. You just need the secret recipe. So, here you go. **Serves 2 to 4**

1½ pounds (680 g) russet potatoes, peeled (or skin-on for rustic style)

2 tablespoons (30 ml) white vinegar

Sea salt

¾ teaspoon garlic powder

¾ teaspoon onion powder

½ teaspoon smoked paprika

½ teaspoon freshly ground black pepper

4 to 6 cups (960 ml to 1.4 L) peanut oil or high-heat fryer oil blend

2 teaspoons grated Parmesan cheese

Malt vinegar, optional

Optional dipping sauces for serving: garlic aioli, spicy ketchup, chipotle mayo, or ranch dressing.

1. Cut the potatoes into ¼-inch to ½-inch-thick (6 mm to 12 mm) fries (classic bar-cut).
2. Fill a large bowl three-quarters full of cold water. Swish in the white vinegar. Soak the potatoes for at least 30 minutes, and up to 1 hour. Drain, rinse, and pat completely dry with paper towels.
3. In a small bowl, whisk together all the spices. Set aside. In a large Dutch oven or a fryer, heat the oil to 300°F (150°C). Line a baking sheet with paper towels.
4. Fry the potatoes in batches, for 4 to 5 minutes, or until pale and tender, but not browned. Use a slotted spoon to transfer them to the prepared tray. Let rest for at least 10 minutes.
5. Increase the heat to 375°F (190°C). Fry the potatoes again, in batches, for 2 to 4 minutes or until deep golden brown and crisp. Transfer to a baking sheet and sprinkle with the seasoning blend.
6. Dust with the cheese. Toss to coat. Serve in a lined bar basket or dish, with malt vinegar or whatever dipping sauces you prefer, on the side.

Maple-Roasted Carrots for Two

Sometimes the night and the meal call for something delicately sweet, like love itself. The perfect symphony of simple flavor and texture makes this dish more than the sum of its limited parts. For something from the ground, it would be right at home at the top of the world, on the table for an intimate meal between Scott and Kip in Scott's sky-high apartment. Although an adaptable side, it would go especially well with the steak on page 91. **Serves 2**

1½ tablespoons (23 ml) pure maple syrup

1 tablespoon (15 ml) fresh orange juice

1 tablespoon (15 ml) olive oil

½ teaspoon ground cinnamon

⅓ teaspoon sea salt

¼ teaspoon freshly ground black pepper

1 pound (454 g) rainbow or heirloom carrots, peeled and cut on the bias

1 tablespoon (12 g) chopped toasted pumpkin seeds

1. Preheat the oven to 425°F (220°C). Line a baking sheet with parchment paper.
2. In a large bowl, whisk together the maple syrup, orange juice, oil, cinnamon, salt, and pepper. Add the carrots and toss thoroughly until evenly coated.
3. Spread the carrots out in a single layer on the baking sheet. Roast for 20 to 30 minutes, turning once halfway through, until fork tender and beginning to brown.
4. Transfer to a warm serving dish and sprinkle with the pumpkin seeds. Serve warm. Refrigerate leftover carrots in a sealed container for up to 3 days.

36
36

Slapshot Biscuits

Excuse the name. It's a bit ironic, because these are entirely the opposite of the rock-hard pucks that fly off the stick blades wielded by masters Hollander, Rozanov, Barrett, and Hunter. The moniker comes from the fact that the delicate pillowy softness and delightful tang of these butter-holding clouds are so incredibly good that you want to get them to your goalie as fast as possible. (Eric, you've been warned.)

Makes 10 to 12 biscuits

- 2½ cups (300 g) all-purpose flour, plus more for dusting
- 1 tablespoon (12 g) granulated sugar
- 1 tablespoon (12 g) baking powder
- ½ teaspoon baking soda
- 1 teaspoon sea salt
- ¾ cup (170 g) cold unsalted butter, cubed or grated
- 1 cup (240 ml) cold buttermilk, plus more as needed
- 2 tablespoons (28 g) unsalted butter, melted
- Butter, honey, preserves, or clotted cream, optional for serving

1. Preheat the oven to 425°F (220°C). Line a baking sheet with parchment paper.
2. In a large bowl, whisk together the flour, sugar, baking powder and soda, and salt until evenly mixed.
3. Cut in the cold butter using a pastry cutter or your fingers until the mixture resembles coarse crumbs with pea-size butter pieces.
4. Pour in the buttermilk and stir gently with a fork until the dough just comes together. Do not overmix; the dough should look slightly shaggy.
5. Turn the dough out onto a lightly floured surface. Pat into a rectangle about 1 inch (2.5 cm) thick. Fold into thirds like a letter. Rotate 90 degrees and roll out. Repeat the fold two more times, rotating after each folding.
6. Roll the dough out to 1-inch (2.5 cm) thick and cut out biscuits using a floured biscuit cutter. (Do not twist the cutter.) Gather the scraps, reroll, and cut out more biscuits.
7. Arrange on the baking sheet. For soft-sided biscuits, the sides should touch; leave space for crisp sides. Brush tops with melted butter.
8. Bake 18 to 22 minutes, or until deep golden brown on top. Remove from oven and brush again with butter. Let rest for 5 minutes.
9. Serve warm with desired side. Store leftover biscuits in a sealed container at room temperature for up to 2 days, or freeze for up to 2 months.

526-332

The Waiter's-Crash Canapés

Kip makes a great boyfriend, and he could certainly blend up a mean smoothie, but he never really had the chops as a catering waiter. Running into Scott at a charity event was a literal "crash" course in how not to carry a tray of canapés with style (but it certainly helped endear Kip to Scott). The fresh and flavorful ingredients in this recipe honor whatever might be simmering between you and your crush—but do keep these on ice until ready to serve. **Makes 24 canapés**

1 pound (454 g) large shrimp, peeled, deveined, tails removed

¾ cup (180 ml) fresh lime juice

½ cup (62 g) diced English cucumber

¼ cup (36 g) finely diced red onion

1 small jalapeño, seeded and minced

1 tablespoon (15 ml) extra-virgin olive oil

½ teaspoon sea salt, plus more for water

¼ teaspoon white pepper

⅓ cup (50 g) finely diced ripe avocado

2 tablespoons (6 g) chopped fresh dill

1 tablespoon (3 g) sliced fresh chives

3 or 4 heads Belgian endive

Freshly ground black pepper

Flaky sea salt

1. Fill a large heatproof bowl with a half-and-half mixture of ice and water. Bring a medium saucepan of salted water to a gentle boil over medium-high heat.
2. Poach the shrimp for 2 to 3 minutes, or until just turning pink and opaque and beginning to curl. Transfer them immediately to the ice bath. Let them cool completely, then drain and pat dry.
3. Dice the shrimp into ¼-inch (6 mm) pieces. Transfer to a bowl with the lime juice and stir until completely coated. Cover and refrigerate for 15 minutes.
4. Drain. To shrimp, add the cucumber, onion, jalapeño, oil, salt, and white pepper. Gently fold in the avocado, dill, and chives and refrigerate for 15 minutes.
5. Separate the endive leaves carefully and select the crispest boat-shaped spears. Rinse them and pat dry.
6. Arrange the spears on a chilled serving platter and spoon 1 tablespoon of shrimp ceviche into each one. Dust with black pepper and flaky sea salt. Serve immediately. Refrigerate leftover ceviche in a sealed container for up to 24 hours.

All-Star Game Mango Salsa
and Homemade Pita Chips

Only the best make it onto the ice of an All-Star Game. It's a chance to join the elite and thrill the crowd—and afterward, a chance to sneak away for some private time with your beau. Ilya and Shane played five All-Star Games as competitors before they got to play on the same team, so to speak, in Tampa Bay. After a winning game, a very public celebratory kiss on the cheek, and a tender moment on the beach, they retreated behind closed doors. This requires a snack that rises to the occasion. This version of humble salsa and chips makes the grade, with mango adding a sweet, cooling twist to the traditionally acidic and salty flavors. **Serves 6**

3 ripe mangoes, peeled and finely diced
½ cup (72 g) diced red bell pepper
¼ cup (28 g) minced red onion
1 jalapeño, seeded and minced
¼ cup (4 g) fresh cilantro, finely chopped
Juice of 2 limes
1 teaspoon sea salt, divided
¼ teaspoon freshly ground black pepper
12 small pitas
3 tablespoons (45 ml) vegetable oil or avocado oil

Save time by swapping the pita chips for blue-corn tortilla chips, if desired.

1. In a medium bowl, combine the fruit and vegetables, cilantro, and lime juice. Toss to coat. Season with salt and pepper. Cover and refrigerate for 15 to 20 minutes.
2. Preheat the oven to 375°F (190°C). Line 2 baking sheets with parchment paper.
3. Stack pitas and cut into 6 wedges each. Transfer to a large bowl, drizzle with oil, and sprinkle liberally with salt. Toss until evenly coated.
4. Arrange the wedges in a single layer on the baking sheets. Bake for 10 to 12 minutes, turning once halfway through, until golden and crisp. Remove from the oven and let cool completely on the baking sheets.
5. Transfer the mango salsa to a serving bowl and arrange the chips in a basket. Serve immediately. Refrigerate leftover salsa in a sealed container for up to 3 days. The chips can be kept for up to 5 days at room temperature in a tightly sealed plastic bag or container.

Game-Day Dip, Three Ways

This trio of legendary dips honors the trio of legendary hockey talents that headline the *Heated Rivalry* series—Shane, Ilya, and Scott. Like the stars themselves, each dip has its own charms and quirks. You choose which star represents which dip. Doesn't really matter; like the stars themselves, the dips are all yummy and addictive. Enjoy them with tortilla chips, pita chips (page 69), vegetable crudités, or whatever dip-delivery system you prefer. **Serves 6 to 8**

FOR THE HUMMUS

1 can (15.5 ounces, or 439 g) chickpeas, drained and rinsed

¼ cup (60 g) tahini

2 tablespoons (30 ml) lemon juice

1½ tablespoons (23 ml) extra-virgin olive oil

1 or 2 cloves garlic

½ teaspoon ground cumin

FOR THE BABA GHANOUSH

2 medium eggplants

2 tablespoons (28 g) tahini

1½ tablespoons (23 ml) lemon juice

1½ tablespoons (23 ml) extra-virgin olive oil

2 cloves garlic

½ teaspoon ground cumin

FOR THE GUACAMOLE

3 large ripe avocados, halved and pitted

3 tablespoons (23 g) minced red onion

2 cloves garlic, minced

1 small jalapeño, seeded and minced

2 tablespoons (30 ml) lime juice

1½ tablespoons (5 g) chopped fresh cilantro

FOR THE HUMMUS

Combine all the ingredients in a food processor. Blend until thick and smooth. Drizzle in cold water while blending as needed until the hummus is creamy. Taste, and add more lemon juice or salt as needed.

FOR THE BABA GHANOUSH

1. Preheat the oven to 425°F (220°C). Line a baking sheet with aluminum foil.
2. Prick the eggplants all over with a knife and place them on the baking sheet. Roast for 35 to 40 minutes, turning once, until collapsed and the skin is charred.
3. Cool the eggplant slightly. Cut in half lengthwise and scoop out the flesh. Drain the flesh in a sieve for 10 minutes.
4. Transfer to a food processor with the remaining ingredients. Pulse until you achieve desired texture. Taste, and add lemon juice or salt and ground black pepper as needed.

FOR THE GUACAMOLE

In a medium bowl, mash the avocado flesh with a fork, leaving it slightly chunky. Add the remaining ingredients. Taste, and add salt and more lime juice as needed.

Spoon each dip into separate shallow bowls. Create divots in the center of each with the back of a spoon, and drizzle in extra-virgin olive oil to taste. Refrigerate leftover dips tightly covered (press plastic wrap to the surface of the guacamole), for up to 5 days.

04

HOME TEAM DINNERS

Successful hockey franchises like those in Montreal, New York, Boston, or Ottawa are, by another name, families. Teammates sometimes butt heads and argue, but they always come together when it matters. They share their victories and their defeats, no matter how small or large.

Shane Hollander leads Montreal as a deeply close unit, because his small family has always been a tight-knit source of support to him. He treats his teammates, guys like Hayden Pike and J.J. Boiziau, as brothers, not just coworkers. Ilya Rozanov and Scott Hunter lead their teams in similar ways. They have an especially powerful sense of family because both have suffered the heartbreak of losing loved ones. So, they hold together their teams as if they shared DNA.

Call it a team or call it family; it's all about community. The important part is that everyone supports one another. Each person gives the others room to be who they are, while still loving and respecting them. It's about sharing much more than ice time.

That includes meals.

Team dinners, like family dinners, are special occasions. Gathering as one to share good food inspires better conversation and spawns wonderful forever memories. That's a lot to ask from a meal. And it's why the dinners in this chapter have been so thoughtfully crafted.

Dinners can include the whole team, or just the few who have time in their schedule. They are still precious and the food has to reflect that. It's why you'll find dishes like the penne alla vodka on page 75 that can feed a crowd, and smaller portions like the tomato soup and grilled cheese on page 95—more modest, but no less satisfying.

Smaller gatherings can be just as heartwarming, loud, and raucous. But large or small, shared dinners are about just *being* with one another. Being ourselves, being teammates, being friends, and even being lovers.

So plan the meal, call your people, and set the table. It's time to ring the dinner bell.

LOVE+LOVE+LOVE+LOVE+
LOVE+LOVE+LOVE+LOVE+

Out and About Penne alla Vodka

Here's an interpretation of the meal at the center of one of the most heartwarming moments in *Heated Rivalry*. After Shane returns with Ilya to his parents' cabin to formally come out (after David has seen the couple), everyone sits down to a dinner of Yuna's spaghetti. As somber as things appear, Ilya tucks right in, having found love, family, and a tasty dinner, all at once. You and yours will have the same reaction to this satisfying dish—made with the more traditional penne, and Russian flare. **Serves 6**

1½ pounds (680 g) penne

5 tablespoons (70 g) unsalted butter, divided

2 tablespoons (30 ml) extra-virgin olive oil

1 medium sweet onion, minced

1 tablespoon (15 g) minced garlic

3 tablespoons (50 g) double-concentrated tomato paste

1 cup (252 g) crushed San Marzano tomatoes

¾ cup (180 ml) Russian vodka

1 cup (240 ml) heavy whipping cream

½ cup (50 g) freshly grated Parmigiano-Reggiano, plus extra for serving

Sea salt to taste, plus more for pasta water

Freshly ground black pepper

2 tablespoons (6 g) sliced fresh basil

1. Bring a large pot of heavily salted water to a boil over high heat. Add the penne and cook to al dente according to package directions, 9 to 12 minutes. (Test the pasta regularly to avoid overcooking.)
2. Drain and set aside, reserving 1 cup (240 ml) of the pasta water.
3. In a large skillet over medium heat, melt 3 tablespoons (42 g) of butter with the olive oil. Add the onion and cook for 6 to 8 minutes, or until soft and translucent. Stir in the garlic and cook for 1 minute. Add the tomato paste and cook for 3 to 4 minutes, stirring constantly, until the paste deepens in color.
4. Stir in the tomatoes and simmer for 5 minutes. Add the vodka and simmer for 6 to 8 minutes, stirring occasionally, until the sauce reduces slightly.
5. Reduce the heat to medium-low; stir in the cream until incorporated. Simmer for 5 minutes, or until the sauce is silky and pink.
6. Stir in the cheese. Taste, and add salt and pepper as needed. Simmer for 2 to 3 minutes, or until the cheese is melted and the sauce is smooth.
7. Add the penne and gently toss until coated. Add the remaining butter and a splash of the reserved pasta water, as needed, to thin the sauce.
8. Transfer to individual serving bowls, top with the basil and a sprinkle of cheese, and serve. Refrigerate leftover pasta for up to 4 days, reheating with a splash of cream.

Steak-a-Bobs for Sharing

When your sport gives you summers off, you learn to love a good grilled meal. That's why hockey stars from Ryan to Troy to Scott deeply appreciate a good cookout. You don't have to have a cottage on a lake to understand the pleasure of a casual backyard meal. And few summer meals are as wonderful hot off the grill as juicy cubes of meat and perfectly grilled veggies; it makes for hot-weather-heaven on a plate. **Serves 6**

⅓ cup (80 ml) plus ¼ cup (60 ml) soy sauce, divided

½ cup (120 ml) balsamic vinegar, divided

5 tablespoons (75 ml) olive oil, divided

2 tablespoons (27 g) light brown sugar

4 teaspoons minced garlic

1 tablespoon chopped fresh rosemary

2½ pounds (1.1 kg) sirloin or ribeye, cut into 2-inch (5 cm) cubes

2 large red bell peppers, seeded and cut into 2-inch (5 cm) pieces

2 large yellow bell peppers, seeded and cut into 2-inch (5 cm) pieces

1 large red onion, cut into wedges

2 zucchinis, cut into thick slices

1 pound (454 g) cremini or button mushrooms, trimmed

1 pint cherry tomatoes

Sea salt

Freshly ground black pepper

2 tablespoons (42 g) honey

1 tablespoon (14 g) unsalted butter

1. In a large mixing bowl with lid, or gallon-size resealable bag, combine ⅓ cup (80 ml) soy sauce, ¼ cup (60 ml) vinegar, 2 tablespoons (30 ml) olive oil, sugar, garlic, and rosemary. Add the meat and toss until coated. Cover or seal and refrigerate for at least 2 hours, preferably overnight.
2. Preheat the grill on medium-high, leaving one side on low heat.
3. In a large bowl, toss all the vegetables with 2 tablespoons (30 ml) olive oil and season with salt and pepper. Thread the veggies onto skewers.
4. Remove the meat, pat dry with paper towels, then toss with 1 tablespoon (15 ml) oil. Thread the cubes onto heavy skewers, leaving space between the pieces.
5. Grill the vegetables on the hot side of the grill for 12 to 14 minutes, turning until lightly charred and tender. For medium-rare meat skewers, place next to the hot side of the grill for 5 to 6 minutes. Move to the higher-heat side to finish cooking for 4 to 6 minutes. Transfer all the skewers to a platter and tent loosely with foil.
6. Meanwhile, in a small saucepan over medium heat, combine ¼ cup (60 ml) soy sauce, ¼ cup (60 ml) vinegar, honey, and butter. Bring to a simmer and stir until butter is melted.
7. Arrange hot skewers on a large platter. Brush lightly with the sauce; serve remaining sauce on the side. Refrigerate leftovers for up to 3 days.

Iron Curtain Borscht

Want to press your lips to Ilya's? Feel those rippling muscles as he holds you close? Well, unfortunately (spoiler alert), he's fictional. The next best thing is to taste the heart of Mother Russia. That's what this borscht delivers: a soup that eats like a meal and captures the heartiness and humor of the true Russian spirit. Not the hatred and bigotry of Ilya's father and brother, but the wit, compassion, and love of Ilya and his mother, Irina. **Serves 6**

- 4 tablespoons (56 g) unsalted butter, divided
- 3 medium beets, peeled and grated
- 2 tablespoons (33 g) tomato paste
- 1 can (15 ounces, or 425 g) crushed tomatoes
- 1 teaspoon smoked paprika
- 2 tablespoons (30 ml) olive oil
- 2 medium yellow onions, diced
- 3 cloves garlic, minced
- 2 large carrots, julienned
- 2 medium parsnips, julienned
- 2 cups (140 g) shredded green cabbage
- 8 cups (1.9 L) vegetable stock
- 2 large Yukon Gold potatoes, peeled and diced
- 2 tablespoons (30 ml) red wine vinegar
- 1 tablespoon (15 ml) lemon juice
- 1 tablespoon (12 g) granulated sugar
- 1 teaspoon dried dill
- Sea salt
- Freshly ground black pepper
- 6 slices dark rye bread
- 3 tablespoons (42 g) salted butter, softened
- Sour cream
- Fresh dill sprigs, for garnish

1. In a large skillet over medium-high heat, melt 1 tablespoon (14 g) unsalted butter. Cook beets for 6 minutes. Stir in tomato paste and cook for 2 minutes.
2. Add tomatoes and paprika. Simmer for 10 minutes, or until beets are fork tender. Set aside.
3. In a large stockpot over medium heat, combine the remaining unsalted butter and olive oil. Add onions and sauté for 8 to 10 minutes or until soft. Stir in garlic and cook for 1 minute more.
4. Add the carrots and parsnips and cook for 5 minutes. Stir in cabbage and cook for 5 minutes more.
5. Add stock and bring to a gentle boil. Add potatoes; reduce heat to low. Simmer 25 to 30 minutes, until potatoes are fork tender.
6. Stir in beets, vinegar, lemon juice, sugar, and dried dill. Season to taste with salt and pepper. Let soup rest for 15 minutes. Preheat oven to 375°F (190°C).
7. Brush bread with salted butter and sprinkle with salt. Cut slices into triangles; arrange on baking sheet. Toast for 8 to 10 minutes, until crisp.
8. Ladle soup into deep bowls. Top with a generous dollop of sour cream, fresh dill, and toast points. Refrigerate leftovers in a sealed container for up to 5 days, or freeze for up to 3 months.

MVP Sheet-Pan Thighs
to Die For

Can you blame Kip, Svetlana, Kyle, or Rose? Really, how can any person with a pulse not lust after the hard bodies that populate professional hockey? (Honestly, have you seen Scott Hunter in his underwear?) Much as you can crave the buns of steel and abs to die for, hockey players are more justly famous for their swole, rock-hard . . . thighs. They've got thighs like nobody's business. This dish is an homage featuring the less-impressive but no-less-delicious versions from the local chicken ranch. **Serves 4 to 6**

8 bone-in, skin-on chicken thighs
¼ cup (60 ml) olive oil, divided
1 tablespoon (30 g) Dijon mustard
1 teaspoon smoked paprika
1 teaspoon sea salt, divided
1 teaspoon freshly ground black pepper, divided
1½ pounds (680 g) fingerling potatoes, halved lengthwise
1 large red onion, cut into wedges
4 cloves garlic, smashed
1 lemon, thinly sliced
1 tablespoon (3 g) chopped fresh parsley

1. Preheat the oven to 425°F (220°C). Pat the chicken dry with paper towels.
2. In a large bowl, whisk together 2 tablespoons (30 ml) olive oil, mustard, paprika, and ½ teaspoon each salt and pepper. Add the chicken thighs and massage the marinade under and over the skin. Marinate at room temperature for 20 minutes, or refrigerate for up to 8 hours.
3. Place potatoes, onions, and garlic on a large baking sheet. Drizzle with 2 tablespoons (30 ml) oil. Season with ½ teaspoon each salt and pepper. Toss to coat.
4. Nestle the chicken thighs skin-side up among the vegetables in a single layer. Arrange the lemon slices around and beneath the chicken.
5. Roast for 40 to 50 minutes, or until the chicken reaches an internal temperature of 175°F (80°C), the skin is deep golden brown and crispy, and the potatoes are fork tender.
6. Sprinkle with the parsley and serve family style while hot. Refrigerate leftovers in a sealed container for up to 4 days.

Miso-Glazed Salmon Grain Bowls

Throughout the *Heated Rivalry* series, we see Shane eating healthy, whether he's out with his parents or dining at Hayden's, claiming he can't relax his regimen for even one day during hockey season. By the time we get to book 6, *The Long Game*, Shane is on such a strict diet that even Ilya can't understand it . . . until he decides to try. He searches for a recipe suitable for them to cook together, which Shane finds incredibly romantic. And the dish wasn't too bad either—even Ilya approved. Give this version a try and see for yourself. Then think about what you'll have for dessert. **Serves 4**

- 4 (6-ounce, or 170 g) skin-on salmon fillets
- 3 tablespoons (54 g) white miso paste
- 2 tablespoons (30 ml) mirin
- 1½ tablespoons (23 ml) soy sauce or tamari
- 1½ tablespoons (23 ml) pure maple syrup or honey
- 1 tablespoon (15 ml) rice vinegar
- 1 teaspoon grated ginger
- ¼ teaspoon freshly ground black pepper, plus more as needed
- 1 cup (208 g) uncooked pearled farro
- 3 cups (720 ml) water or vegetable broth
- 1 teaspoon sea salt, divided
- 2 cups (226 g) cauliflower florets
- 1 cup (85 g) broccoli florets
- 1 red bell pepper, sliced
- 1 cup (42 g) shredded or ribboned carrots
- 2 tablespoons (30 ml) olive oil
- 2 scallions, thinly sliced on a bias
- 1 tablespoon (9 g) toasted sesame seeds
- Lime wedges

1. Pat salmon dry with paper towels. Place in a shallow baking dish.
2. In a small bowl, whisk together miso, mirin, soy sauce, syrup or honey, vinegar, ginger, and black pepper until smooth. Spoon over fish. Marinate for 15 to 20 minutes at room temperature, or up to 1 hour refrigerated.
3. Rinse farro under cold water until the water runs clear. Transfer to a medium saucepan with water or broth and ½ teaspoon salt. Bring to a boil over medium-high heat, reduce to low, cover, and simmer for 22 to 25 minutes, until tender but pleasantly chewy. Fluff with a fork and keep warm. Preheat oven to 425°F (220°C). Line a baking sheet with parchment paper.
4. In a medium bowl, toss vegetables with olive oil, ½ teaspoon salt, and pepper to taste. Spread evenly on the baking sheet.
5. Roast for 15 minutes. Remove from the oven. Reduce temperature to 400°F (205°C).
6. Stir vegetables and push to the sides. Place salmon skin-side down in the center. Spoon glaze over. Roast for 10 to 12 minutes more, or until salmon is just cooked through and lightly caramelized.
7. Divide farro among 4 shallow bowls. Top with vegetables and a salmon fillet. Garnish with scallions and sesame seeds and serve with lime wedges. Refrigerate components separately in sealed containers for up to 3 days.

Tourtière Mon Amour

If there were a recipe for the many flavors of beefcake, you'd find it in the Game Changers series of books. But this meaty portable meal is probably as close as you'll come to an actual beefcake recipe. (Or beef pie, as it were.) The name translates to "Meat pie, my love," and the dish is a specialty of Shane Hollander's team's home turf of Quebec. It's sure to satisfy any meat-eater's appetite. **Makes 10 to 12 pies**

3 cups (360 g) all-purpose flour, plus more for dusting

2 teaspoons sea salt, divided

1 tablespoon (12 g) granulated sugar

1¼ cups (282 g) cold unsalted butter, cubed

7 to 9 tablespoons (105 to 135 ml) ice water

2 tablespoons (28 g) unsalted butter

1 large sweet onion, minced

1 tablespoon (15 g) minced garlic

1 pound (454 g) ground pork

1 pound (454 g) ground beef

1 Yukon Gold potato, peeled and diced into ¼-inch (6 mm) cubes

½ cup (120 ml) beef or chicken stock

½ teaspoon freshly ground black pepper

1 teaspoon dried savory

½ teaspoon dried thyme

½ teaspoon ground cinnamon

1 large egg

1 teaspoon milk

1. In a large bowl, whisk together flour, 1 teaspoon salt, and sugar. Cut in cold butter using a pastry cutter or your fingers until mixture resembles coarse crumbs. Drizzle in ice water, a bit at a time, mixing until the dough comes together. Divide into 2 disks, wrap tightly, and refrigerate at least 45 minutes.
2. Melt 2 tablespoons (28 g) butter in a large skillet over medium heat. Add onion and cook for 8 minutes until soft. Add garlic; cook for 1 minute more.
3. Add meats and cook, breaking into fine crumbles, until no longer pink, about 10 minutes.
4. Stir in potato, stock, and spices (including remaining 1 teaspoon salt). Simmer for 20 to 25 minutes, stirring occasionally, until potatoes are fork tender and sauce is thick. Transfer to a large baking pan and cool completely.
5. Preheat the oven to 400°F (200°C) with a rack in lower third. Line 2 baking sheets with parchment paper.
6. Roll out the dough on a lightly floured surface to about ⅛-inch (3 mm) thick. Cut into 6-inch (15 cm) rounds. Scoop ⅓ cup (36 g) filling slightly off-center on each.
7. Brush edges with water and fold dough over filling to form half-moons. Press edges firmly, then crimp with a fork.
8. Transfer to baking sheets and cut a small steam vent in each. Refrigerate 15 minutes.
9. Whisk together egg and milk. Brush over the pies. Bake 20 minutes. Lower temperature to 375°F (190°C) and bake 15 to 20 minutes more, until the crusts are deep golden brown and crispy.
10. Let rest 10 minutes before serving. Refrigerate leftover pies in a sealed container up to 4 days, or freeze up to 2 months.

A Quiche Before You Go

Date a hockey player and, sooner or later, you discover that you're going to deal with the wake-up call for early morning practice. You want to give him something special and low-carb before he heads out the door (no, not that something special . . . something to eat . . . no, not *that* something to eat, either), but there isn't time to cook a hot breakfast. That's where this crustless, rich, filling, and make-ahead meal-in-a-pie-pan comes in. On days off from training, it's the perfect centerpiece for a lazy brunch. **Serves 6 to 8**

2 tablespoons (28 g) unsalted butter
8 ounces (227 g) thick-cut bacon, diced
2 large shallots, sliced fine
1 small sweet onion, diced
½ teaspoon fresh thyme leaves
Freshly ground black pepper
4 large eggs
1½ cups (360 ml) heavy whipping cream
½ teaspoon sea salt
¼ teaspoon white pepper
1 cup (113 g) grated Gruyère cheese
1 tablespoon (3 g) chopped fresh chives

1. Preheat the oven to 350°F (175°C). Generously grease a 9-inch (23-cm) deep-dish pie or ceramic quiche dish with the butter and place on a baking sheet. Line a plate with paper towels.
2. In a large skillet over medium heat, cook the bacon until crisp. Transfer it with a slotted spoon to the prepared plate.
3. Discard the excess fat from the pan, leaving about 1 tablespoon (15 ml). Add the shallots and onion, and sauté for 6 to 8 minutes, or until soft and slightly caramelized.
4. Stir in the thyme and pepper, and cook 1 minute more. Remove from heat and add the bacon. Let cool while you make the custard.
5. In a large bowl, whisk together the eggs, cream, salt, and white pepper until integrated.
6. Sprinkle the Gruyère evenly in the baking dish. Spoon the bacon mix over the cheese, and pour in the custard. Bake for 35 to 40 minutes, or until the custard is just set at the center but still slightly wobbly. If the top starts burning, tent loosely with foil.
7. Turn off the oven and let the quiche rest inside with the door ajar for 5 minutes.
8. Cool on a wire rack for 15 to 20 minutes before slicing. Garnish with the chives and serve warm. Refrigerate leftover quiche, tightly covered, for up to 5 days.
9. Reheat in a 325°F (165°C) oven, covered loosely with foil, for 15 to 25 minutes until warmed through. For a quick option, microwave slices in 30-second intervals, but the texture will be softer.

First Date Shakshuka

Just about every culture around the world has its own version of shakshuka. This more traditional version is a one-pan wonder that will feed a crowd at brunch, and can easily double as the perfect casual dinner for the entire home team. Or, if you're like Eric Bennett, you'll make this for your sweetie, eat it straight out of the pan, and see where the night takes you. **Serves 4**

- 2 tablespoons (30 ml) extra-virgin olive oil, plus more as needed
- 1 large yellow onion, diced
- 1 large red bell pepper, seeded and diced
- 1 tablespoon (15 g) minced garlic
- 1 teaspoon ground cumin
- 1 teaspoon smoked paprika
- 1 tablespoon (17 g) tomato paste
- 1 can (28 ounces, or 796 g) crushed San Marzano tomatoes
- 1 teaspoon granulated sugar or honey
- ¾ teaspoon sea salt, plus more as needed
- ½ teaspoon freshly ground black pepper, plus more as needed
- 8 large eggs
- ½ cup (56 g) crumbled feta cheese
- ¼ cup (15 g) chopped fresh parsley
- Warm pita or grilled sourdough
- Chili oil, optional

You can easily halve this recipe to serve 2 by using a 15-ounce (425 g) can of tomatoes and a medium skillet.

1. In a 12-inch (30 cm) skillet or sauté pan over medium heat, heat the oil. Add the onion and cook for 5 to 7 minutes, or until soft and translucent.
2. Stir in the bell pepper and cook for 4 to 5 minutes, or until slightly tender. Add the garlic and cook for 1 minute more.
3. Stir in the cumin and paprika, and cook for 30 to 45 seconds. Stir in the tomato paste and cook 1 to 2 minutes more, or until the color starts to deepen.
4. Add the tomatoes, sugar, salt, and black pepper. Bring to a simmer and cook uncovered for 12 to 15 minutes, stirring occasionally, until thickened.
5. Reduce the heat to low and use the back of a large spoon to create 8 small wells in the sauce. Crack an egg into each well and season lightly with salt and pepper.
6. Cover the skillet and cook for 5 to 8 minutes. The whites should be set and the yolks should remain soft and runny.
7. Sprinkle with feta and parsley. Serve in the pan, family style with bread on the side. Drizzle lightly with olive oil or chili oil, if desired. Refrigerate leftover sauce in a sealed container for up to 4 days.

84

Steak au Frites for Two

As Ilya and Shane proved on more than one occasion, a luxury hotel suite is ideal for a memorable, under-the-radar, rough-and-tumble rendezvous. Of course, a guy works up a healthy appetite in those circumstances, and what better way to satisfy than a little meat, properly cooked and delivered right to your door? This is a perfect and luxurious way to cook a steak, and makes for a forever-memorable meal **Serves 2**

2 large russet potatoes, peeled

1 tablespoon (15 ml) white vinegar

4 cups (960 ml) neutral frying oil (peanut, canola, or sunflower)

2 ribeye or sirloin steaks (10 to 12 ounces, or 283 to 340 g) 1¼-inch (3.2 cm) thick

Sea salt

1 tablespoon (15 ml) avocado oil

Freshly ground black pepper

2 tablespoons (28 g) unsalted butter

2 cloves garlic, crushed

1. Cut potatoes into ¼-inch (6 mm) sticks. Fill a large bowl three-quarters full with the water and stir in the vinegar. Soak potatoes for 30 minutes. Drain; dry with paper towels.
2. In a deep skillet, heat the frying oil to 325°F (165°C). Line a baking sheet with paper towels.
3. Working in batches, fry potatoes for 4 to 5 minutes, or until pale and tender but not brown. Remove to the baking sheet and let rest for 15 minutes.
4. Increase oil temperature to 375°F (190°C). Preheat oven to 200°F (95°C). Remove the steaks from the refrigerator 30 minutes before cooking.
5. Fry potatoes again for 2 to 3 minutes per batch, or until golden brown and crispy. Remove, drain on baking sheet, and season immediately with sea salt. Keep warm in the oven while you cook the steaks.
6. Heat a cast-iron skillet over high heat until smoking, and add the avocado oil. Pat steaks dry and season generously with salt and pepper.
7. Sear steaks without moving for 3 to 4 minutes. Flip and sear other side for 3 minutes.
8. Reduce heat to medium. Add butter and crushed garlic. Tilt the skillet and baste steaks continuously for 1 to 2 minutes.
9. Cook the steaks to an internal temperature of 125°F to 128°F (52°C to 53°C) for medium-rare, or 130°F to 135°F (54°C to 57°C) for medium. (They will continue to cook for a short time after being removed from the heat.)
10. Rest steaks for 8 to 10 minutes before slicing against the grain, or serve whole, with frites piled on the side.

The Captain's Chicken Kiev

When it comes to culinary trends, everything old is new again! This is a dish that Ilya's father, Grigori, likely enjoyed at many a policemen's banquet in Moscow; now it has found its way into this lineup—in a slightly updated version. That shouldn't come as a surprise because the Russians are fond of a hearty, filling meal, and this is a delicious upgrade over plain-old roast chicken breast. **Serves 4**

- 1 cup (226 g) unsalted butter, softened
- 1 tablespoon (15 g) minced garlic
- 2 tablespoons (6 g) finely chopped fresh parsley, plus extra for garnish
- 1 tablespoon (15 ml) lemon juice
- ½ teaspoon sea salt, plus more to season
- 4 (6-ounce, or 170 g) boneless, skinless chicken breasts
- Freshly ground black pepper
- 1 cup (120 g) all-purpose flour
- 3 large eggs, beaten
- 2 cups (120 g) fine bread crumbs or panko
- Vegetable oil
- Lemon wedges

1. In a small bowl, use a fork to combine the butter, garlic, parsley, lemon juice, and salt. Transfer to a sheet of parchment paper. Shape into a log about 1½ inches (4 cm) thick. Freeze for 20 to 30 minutes, or until firm enough to slice.
2. Place each chicken breast between sheets of plastic wrap. Use a meat mallet to pound them to ¼-inch (6 mm) thick. Season both sides lightly with salt and pepper.
3. Slice the chilled butter log into 4 equal patties. Place one in the center of each breast.
4. Fold the sides in, then roll tightly from the bottom to completely contain the butter.
5. Place each breast on a separate piece of plastic wrap. Fold over the sides and twist the ends to form a firm log. Refrigerate for 30 minutes, or until set in the shape.
6. Set up 3 medium, shallow bowls, with the flour, eggs, and bread crumbs, in that order.
7. Unwrap a chicken roll and dredge in the flour, shaking off excess. Dip into the egg wash, and then dredge in the bread crumbs until completely coated. Repeat with all of the rolls. Refrigerate for 15 minutes.
8. In a large, deep skillet, heat 2 inches (5 cm) of oil to 350°F (175°C). Preheat the oven to 375°F (190°C). Set a wire rack in a baking sheet.
9. Carefully lower the chicken into the oil and fry for 4 to 5 minutes per side, or until evenly golden but not fully cooked through. Transfer to the baking sheet; drain completely.
10. Wipe the baking sheet of excess oil and return the rack with the chicken. Bake until the internal temperature reaches 160°F (71°C).
11. Rest chicken for 5 minutes. Serve with lemon wedges and a sprinkle of parsley. Refrigerate leftovers in a sealed container for up to 3 days.

After-Practice Tomato Soup
and Grilled Cheese

It's a good bet that Shane, Ryan, or Eric (or all of them) fondly remember this nostalgic pairing from the snowy days of their youths. What could be more wonderful than coming home exhausted from hockey practice, knowing homework awaited, only to find a steaming bowl of soup and melty, stringy, crunchy sandwiches on the kitchen table? Indulge your own inner ten-year-old by dunking the sandwich in the soup. Mom can't stop you now. **Serves 2**

FOR THE SOUP

6 ripe Roma tomatoes, halved

1 tablespoon (15 ml) olive oil

Sea salt

Freshly ground black pepper

2 tablespoons (28 g) unsalted butter

1 large shallot, diced

1 teaspoon minced garlic

1 tablespoon (17 g) tomato paste

¼ teaspoon smoked paprika

1½ cups (360 ml) chicken or vegetable stock

1 tablespoon (3 g) sliced fresh basil

FOR THE SANDWICHES

4 slices artisanal sourdough or country bread

2 tablespoons (28 g) unsalted butter, softened

1½ cups (168 g) shredded sharp cheddar

MAKE THE SOUP

1. Preheat the oven to 400°F (200°C).
2. Arrange the tomato halves on a small baking sheet, cut-side up. Drizzle with olive oil and season with salt and pepper. Roast for 20 to 25 minutes, or until blistered and browning at the edges.
3. In a medium saucepan over medium heat, melt the butter. Add the shallot and cook for 4 to 5 minutes, or until soft and translucent. Stir in garlic and cook for 30 seconds more.
4. Add tomato paste and cook 1 to 2 minutes until the color begins to deepen. Add tomatoes, juices from the baking sheet, and paprika. Pour in stock and bring to a simmer. Cook 8 to 10 minutes, or just until the mixture begins to thicken.
5. Use an immersion blender, or transfer to a standing blender, to carefully purée the mixture. Return the soup to the saucepan and reduce heat to low. Stir in basil. Add salt and pepper to taste.

MAKE THE SANDWICHES

1. Butter one side of each bread slice. Flip 2 slices over and sprinkle cheese evenly on each. Season with pepper. Top with the remaining slices, butter-side out.
2. Heat a large skillet over medium-low heat. Heat the sandwiches in the skillet for 3 to 4 minutes on each side, or until the bread is golden brown and the cheese is melted.
3. Slice the sandwiches diagonally. Serve with the soup.

Impress-Him Shrimp Scampi

A month into their relationship, Scott and Kip are both all-in, yet still charmingly shy. Neither had been in a serious relationship before, so it's with great anticipation that Scott prepares a Valentine's dinner for Kip—and it's with even greater anticipation that they skip dessert. In culinary terms, "hunter style" means adding mushrooms, so this tasty dish gives you a double dose of Hunter, all while coming together quickly (*ahem*). **Serves 4**

Sea salt

1 pound (454 g) spaghetti

4 ounces (113 g) pancetta, diced

1½ cups (129 g) mixed wild mushrooms (cremini, shiitake, oyster), sliced

1 teaspoon fresh thyme leaves

2 tablespoons (30 ml) olive oil

1½ pounds (680 g) large shrimp, peeled, deveined, tails removed

¼ cup (57 g) unsalted butter

5 cloves garlic, thinly sliced

2 large shallots, minced

½ cup (120 ml) dry white wine

¼ cup (60 ml) dry vermouth

Juice of 1 large lemon

Freshly ground black pepper

3 tablespoons (9 g) chopped fresh parsley

1. Bring a large pot of heavily salted water to a boil over high heat. Cook the spaghetti to al dente, following the package instructions. Drain, reserving 1 cup (240 ml) of water.
2. Heat a large skillet over medium heat. Cook the pancetta until crisp and the fat is rendered, 4 to 5 minutes.
3. Add the mushrooms and cook until golden and any moisture has evaporated. Stir in the thyme. Transfer to a bowl.
4. In the same skillet, heat the olive oil over medium-high heat. Sear the shrimp 1 to 2 minutes per side, or until just pink. Transfer to a plate. Reduce the heat to medium and melt the butter.
5. Add the garlic and shallots. Cook 2 to 3 minutes, or until fragrant and translucent. Deglaze the pan with wine and vermouth, scraping up any browned bits. Simmer for 3 to 4 minutes, or until slightly reduced. Add the lemon juice and season with salt and pepper.
6. Add the spaghetti and about ¼ cup (60 ml) of the reserved pasta water. Toss until the sauce coats the pasta.
7. Add the shrimp and parsley and toss. Twirl the linguini into serving bowls and top with the mushroom mixture. Spoon any extra scampi sauce over top and serve.

Big W Grilled Pork Chops
with Pesto

As Ryan Price would attest, every big hockey victory temporarily satisfies the aching hunger to win. But the Herculean effort of a hallmark win (and a hallmark takedown of opponents) also creates a hunger for, well, food. Filling, satisfying food. Food that honors the triumph. If you're going to win big, you should reward yourself by eating big. A salad? Not so big. These pork chops? Big. Suitably big. And ample enough to share. **Serves 4**

- 4 cups (948 ml) cold water
- 3 tablespoons (54 g) sea salt
- 2 tablespoons (27 g) light brown sugar
- 4 bone-in pork chops (1 to 1½ inches [2.5 to 4 cm] thick)
- 2 packed cups (48 g) basil leaves
- ½ cup (40 g) grated Parmigiano-Reggiano
- 2 cloves garlic
- 6 tablespoons (90 ml) extra-virgin olive oil, divided
- 1 tablespoon (15 ml) lemon juice
- Freshly ground black pepper
- Vegetable oil

1. In a large bowl, whisk together the water, salt, and sugar until dissolved. Submerge the pork chops and refrigerate for 1 hour.
2. Remove the pork chops from the brine, rinse lightly, and pat dry with paper towels.
3. In a food processor, make the pesto. Combine the basil, cheese, and garlic. Pulse until finely chopped.
4. With the motor running, slowly stream in ¼ cup (60 ml) of the olive oil, just until emulsified. Add lemon juice; blend until smooth. Taste and add salt as needed.
5. Brush the pork chops with the remaining 2 tablespoons (30 ml) olive oil and season both sides with salt and pepper. Let stand at room temperature for 20 minutes before grilling.
6. Preheat the grill to medium-high heat (about 400°F to 425°F [205°C to 220°C]). Oil the grates well.
7. Grill chops for 5 to 6 minutes per side, until internal temperature reaches 140°F to 145°F (60°C to 63°C). Transfer chops to a platter and tent loosely with foil. Rest for 5 minutes. Serve topped with the pesto.

Family Meatloaf Meal

Families come in lots of shapes and sizes. The trio of Yuna, Shane, and David. The peewee league team that Hayden Pike is building with his wife. And Kip's family, who welcomes Scott with open arms. Large, small, blended, or not, they all share one essential ingredient: love. More than any spice or protein, that, too, is the most important ingredient in this heartwarming meal that's meant to be shared. **Serves 6 to 8**

FOR THE MEATLOAF

Butter or olive oil for greasing
1 cup (240 ml) whole milk
1 cup (84 g) panko bread crumbs
2 large eggs, lightly beaten
1 medium sweet onion, finely diced
1 tablespoon (15 g) minced garlic
1 cup (272 g) ketchup, divided
2 tablespoons (30 ml) Worcestershire sauce
2 pounds (907 g) ground beef (80% lean)
½ pound (227 g) ground pork
1 teaspoon sea salt
½ teaspoon freshly ground black pepper
2 tablespoons (27 g) light brown sugar
1 tablespoon (15 ml) apple cider vinegar

FOR THE MASHED POTATOES

Sea salt
2 pounds (907 g) new potatoes (halved if large)
3 tablespoons (42 g) unsalted butter
½ cup (120 ml) milk or cream
Freshly ground black pepper

MAKE THE MEATLOAF

1. Preheat the oven to 350°F (175°C). Grease a 9 x 5-inch (23 x 13-cm) loaf pan and line a baking sheet with aluminum foil.
2. In a large bowl, combine the milk and panko; soak for 4 minutes.
3. Add the eggs, onion, garlic, ⅓ cup (91 g) ketchup, and Worcestershire sauce. Stir to combine.
4. Add the meats, salt, and pepper; mix gently by hand until just combined. Do not overmix. Transfer to the loaf pan. Press down so top is level and loaf is firm. Invert over the baking sheet and remove the pan.
5. In a small bowl, whisk together the remaining ketchup, sugar, and vinegar. Brush or pour one-third of the glaze over meatloaf. Bake uncovered for 40 minutes.
6. Remove meatloaf from the oven and brush with one-third of the glaze. Bake for 20 minutes more.
7. Brush meatloaf with the remaining glaze. Bake for 10 to 15 minutes more, or until internal temperature reaches 160°F (71°C). Let rest for 10 to 15 minutes.

MAKE THE MASHED POTATOES

1. While the meatloaf bakes, fill a large pot three-quarters full with cold salted water and add the potatoes. Bring to a boil over medium-high heat. Boil for 15 to 18 minutes, or until fork tender. Drain and return the potatoes to the pot.
2. Add the butter and mash until smooth. Stir in the milk or cream until creamy. Season liberally with salt and pepper.
3. Slice the meatloaf and serve with a healthy scoop of mashed potatoes.

Date Night Chicken Marsala

Life as a couple of champion hunks isn't much different from life as a regular couple—as Shane and Ilya learn. You exchange keys, share dresser drawers, and most definitely host the occasional couples' dinner. When Shane comes out to his teammate Hayden, Hayden is supportive, but not exactly thrilled about Ilya. Shane attempts to mend fences by inviting Hayden and his wife to dinner, trying to forge any type of peace over fabulous coq au vin. This tasty, quicker alternative—served with buttered pasta, mashed potatoes, or rice—is also a good starting point for a détente . . . or just a meal between hunks. **Serves 4**

- 4 (6-ounce [170 g]) boneless, skinless chicken breasts
- Sea salt
- Freshly ground black pepper
- ½ cup (60 g) all-purpose flour
- 4 tablespoons (56 g) unsalted butter, divided
- 2 tablespoons (30 ml) olive oil
- 12 ounces (340 g) cremini or baby bella mushrooms, sliced
- 1 small shallot, finely minced
- 2 teaspoons minced garlic
- ¾ cup (180 ml) dry marsala wine
- ½ cup (120 ml) chicken stock
- 2 teaspoons fresh thyme leaves
- 2 tablespoons (6 g) chopped fresh parsley

1. Slice the chicken breasts horizontally to create thin cutlets. Season both sides of each cutlet with salt and pepper.
2. Spread the flour in a shallow bowl or plate. Lightly dredge the chicken in the flour, shaking off any excess.
3. In a large skillet over medium-high heat, melt 2 tablespoons (28 g) butter with the olive oil. Sear the chicken cutlets for 4 to 5 minutes per side, or until golden brown. (Cook in batches to avoid crowding.) Transfer to a plate and tent loosely with foil.
4. In the same skillet, melt the remaining butter. Add the mushrooms and cook for 6 to 8 minutes, until golden brown.
5. Stir in the shallots and cook for 2 minutes more, or until soft. Add the garlic and cook 30 seconds more.
6. Pour in the marsala, scraping up any browned bits from the pan. Simmer for 3 to 4 minutes, or until the sauce is slightly reduced and glossy.
7. Stir in the chicken stock and thyme. Simmer for 6 to 8 minutes, or until the sauce thickens to a velvety consistency.
8. Return the chicken to the skillet. Spoon sauce over the cutlets while simmering, 4 to 5 minutes, or until the chicken is cooked through. Taste the sauce and add salt and pepper as needed.
9. Transfer the chicken to a serving platter and spoon the sauce over top. Garnish with the parsley.

05

DRINKS WORTHY OF *THE* CUP

The beverages in *Heated Rivalry*, and sprinkled throughout the pages of the books that came before the show, all fall into one of two categories: fuel or fun. The nonalcoholic, healthier versions here are delicious and even meaningful—like Kip's "wink, wink" innuendo of adding a banana to Scott's blueberry smoothie, and Shane's go-to signature ginger ale.

Where the smoothies and nonalcoholic options are about keeping a clear head so that the hockey superstars can take care of business, the boozier options are quite the opposite. Classic intoxicators like the Moscow Mule (anybody thinking that Ilya sometimes plays the jackass?) and the Rookie of the Year are all about boozy hijinks, celebration, and dropping all those pesky inhibitions. Take a sip, kiss who you want, and let the chips fall where they may.

Well, in theory at least.

The drinks in this chapter don't just represent key moments in our beloved characters' lives. They also offer a glimpse into culture, like Ilya's Mother Russia, and context, like the dive-y New York bar with its regular-Joe lineup of cheap beers and sticky banquettes. The booze can set the stage, as the champagne does at the various clubs (let's get wild!) and fundraisers (let's be bored!).

The point is, each flavor-packed drink in this chapter—alcoholic or not—holds meaning. Each possesses its own unique charms. All are worthy of being served in that holy grail of hockey—the Stanley Cup. Just as any hot gay man (and straight woman, for that matter) might be drawn to the hockey player of their dreams, so you, too, will be enticed by these unique and mesmerizing liquid creations.

Crockpot Mulled Cider

Harris Drover, the social media manager for the Ottawa Centaurs, is happy positivity in human form. Newly arrived Troy Barrett is almost the exact opposite, trailing a bad reputation and a scandal with his former team. But Harris isn't about to let Troy wallow in misery. He knows how to spread cheer: a shared evening of holiday wholesomeness and mugs of steaming apple cider made from apples straight out of his family's orchard. This heartwarming, subtly sweet and enticingly spicy concoction captures that moment Harris treats Troy to a joyful snow-globe holiday scene and the possibility of future happiness. **Serves 4 to 6**

4 cinnamon sticks
½ teaspoon whole cloves
8 allspice berries
1 orange, sliced
1 Red Delicious apple, cored and sliced
1-inch (2.5-cm) piece fresh ginger, chopped
½ cup (118 ml) pure maple syrup
6 cups (1.4 L) fresh-pressed apple juice or cider
½ cup (118 ml) merlot, optional
Dried apple or orange slices for serving, optional

1. Add all the ingredients to a slow cooker, including merlot, if using. Cook on low for 4 hours, then keep warm while serving.
2. Spoon into mugs through a sieve or strainer. Garnish with slices of dried apple or orange, if desired.

Mock Mule for Winners

This mocktail is every bit as simple as Shane and Ilya's relationship is complicated. A refreshing alternative to a Moscow Mule, it's also a little like the cocktail called the Ginger Buck—a nickname occasionally given to handsome redheaded hockey players. Shane, though, only has eyes for blondes—one in particular. So, he likes to think of this as a drink in honor of his main competitor and love of his life. It lacks the kick of its namesake, but skip the alcohol and you can go all night. Just like Shane and Ilya. **Serves 1**

8 fresh mint leaves, plus a sprig for garnish

Zest and juice of 2 limes

6 ounces (180 ml) ginger ale

1. In a copper mug, muddle the mint until it's fragrant. Add the lime zest and juice, and fill the mug with ice. Pour the ginger ale slowly over the ice, and use a stir stick to mix the drink.
2. Serve with a sprig of fresh mint.

Flirty Blueberry Smoothie

The most famous smoothie ever to come out of a certain smoothie shop rightly earns the honor. Equal parts epically delicious, nutritious, and satisfying, it has just about everything that a hard body needs to be a hard body: protein, antioxidants, hydration galore, and that extra banana puts it over the top. It was no coincidence that Scott Hunter drank the hell out of this smoothie . . . and went on a winning streak right after. Or that it was the magic spark to Kip and Scott's romance. **Serves 1**

1 cup (133 g) frozen or fresh blueberries

½ cup (70 g) frozen pineapple chunks

2 small bananas, sliced

1 cup (30 g) trimmed and chopped fresh purple kale

1½ cups (356 ml) almond milk

1 tablespoon (16 g) no-sugar-added creamy peanut butter

1 teaspoon raw organic honey

1. Combine all the ingredients in a blender. Pulse until the fruit and veggies are all roughly the same size.
2. Blend on medium for about 30 seconds, or until smooth. Drink immediately.

Rookie of the Year

There is a reason that the Cosmopolitan remains a hugely popular drink. It's a nearly perfect cocktail. Nearly. The only thing better than a Cosmo is a Sparkling Cosmopolitan—which could easily describe one or more of the Admirals in their cosmopolitan city. In this case, though, it's been renamed for the honor Montreal's rookie Shane Hollander earns in his first season. He beat out archrival (and arch something else) Ilya Rozanov to hold the Calder Memorial Trophy. This cocktail is a much more fitting celebration than Shane's regular ginger ale. **Serves 1**

1½ ounces (43 ml) vodka

½ ounce (15 ml) Cointreau

½ ounce (15 ml) lime juice

½ ounce (15 ml) cranberry juice

1½ ounces (43 ml) prosecco or sparkling white wine

Lime wheel, to garnish

1. Combine the vodka, Cointreau, and lime and cranberry juices in a cocktail shaker filled with ice. Shake for about 20 seconds and strain into a chilled martini glass.
2. Top with the prosecco, stir once with a stir stick, garnish with the lime wheel, and serve.

Workout (or Night Out) Recovery Beet & Apple Smoothie

Whether it's post-workout, after a big win against a league rival, or some other (ahem, left unnamed) all-night exertion, you'll need some help on rebounding to your best self the next day. This recovery smoothie has mineral-dense beets, inspired by Ottawa's team captain Ilya, who actively encourages teammate Troy Barrett to recover his love life and go hard after his crush. That crush, Harris, happens to hail from a family of apple farmers—which inspired the addition here of naturally sweet, vitamin-rich apples. **Serves 2**

1 small beet, scrubbed, trimmed, and chopped

1 Granny Smith apple, peeled, cored, and chopped

1 cup (30 g) rinsed and chopped rainbow chard

1 teaspoon chia seeds

1 tablespoon (15 ml) food-grade chilled aloe vera gel

¼ cup (60 ml) kefir

½ cup (120 ml) oat milk

2 or 3 ice cubes

1. Combine all the ingredients in a blender. Pulse until the fruit and veggies are all roughly the same size and the ice has cracked.
2. Blend on medium for about 30 seconds, or until smooth. Drink immediately.

The Bitter Truth

Oh beautiful, tough, sweet, strong Svetlana. Like all of us, she craves love. But she has been attracted to men—like Ilya Rozanov—who can only be dalliances at best and frustrations at worst. This cocktail is based on an old bar-manual standard called Broken and Bitter. In truth, though, Svetlana will never be broken, and she is anything but bitter. Like her, this version is powerful, intoxicating, and so zesty. **Serves 1**

1½ ounces (43 ml) good-quality Russian vodka

½ ounce (15 ml) Campari

1 ounce (30 ml) grapefruit juice

Dash Angostura bitters

½ ounce (15 ml) simple syrup

Quarter wheel pink grapefruit, to garnish

To make simple syrup, add equal parts (by volume) granulated sugar and water to a small saucepan. Heat over medium heat, stirring occasionally, until the sugar dissolves. Remove from heat and cool completely before using. Transfer to a jar, cap, and refrigerate for up to 2 weeks.

1. Combine all liquids in a cocktail shaker filled with ice. Shake for about 20 seconds and strain into a chilled rocks glass.
2. Garnish with the grapefruit wheel and serve.

Northern Lights Julep

You can't play for Montreal without visiting the renowned Gibeau Orange Julep restaurant in the heart of the city. That eatery made famous Canada's version of the creamsicle-flavored smoothie that's called an *orange Julius* in the old US of A. This version adds a little kick to the classic and turns it an alluring green-blue in the process, making it the exact color of the Northern Lights you might see if you were slipping away to, say, the Yukon, to spend some wild time in the wild with your wild boyfriend. **Serves 1**

3 ounces (90 ml) fresh orange juice, chilled

1 small scoop vanilla ice cream

1½ ounces (43 ml) chilled vodka

½ ounce (15 ml) blue curaçao

1½ ounces (43 ml) club soda

1. Combine the orange juice, ice cream, and vodka in a blender. Pulse just until combined, about 3 seconds. Pour into a highball glass.
2. Pour the blue curaçao and club soda on top and slowly stir in, watching as the color changes.

The Canadian Hat Trick

Even if you've read the entire Game Changers series, it's entirely possible you missed what a "hat trick" is: one player scoring three goals in a single hockey game. But what you've certainly not missed is that each book in the series features a hat trick of steamy sex, heady romance, and fast-paced hockey action. This drink offers a fitting celebration of both the hailed hockey feat and the book series' special blend of character chemistry. **Serves 1**

2 ounces (86 ml) Canadian whisky
½ ounce (15 ml) pure maple syrup
2 dashes Angostura bitters
Splash fresh lemon juice
Lemon twist, for garnish

1. Combine the liquids in a cocktail shaker full of ice. Shake for about 20 seconds.
2. Strain into a rocks glass over ice. Garnish with a lemon twist.

Light Up the Net

Troy Barrett was on the down side of bad when he was unceremoniously traded to the bottom-of-the-league Ottawa Centaurs. His rep was in tatters, his teammates didn't want him, and his life was a mess . . . until he got to Ottawa and met Harris Drover. Love has a way of turning things around, just like this cocktail has a way of making any night special. It captures the flavors of a cold and starry night in the Capital City, when the warmth of the drink is like the brush of his fingertips across the top of your hand. **Serves 1**

1 ounce (30 ml) dark rum

½ ounce (15 ml) apple brandy

½ ounce (15 ml) Bénédictine

Splash cinnamon simple syrup

Lemon peel, for garnish

Star anise, for garnish

To make cinnamon simple syrup, follow the directions on page 117, adding 1 or 2 cinnamon sticks to the mixture as it heats. Remove the sticks before refrigerating.

1. Combine all the liquid ingredients in a cocktail shaker full of ice. Shake for about 20 seconds. Strain into a rocks glass over ice.
2. Garnish with a lemon peel and a star anise flower.

Champagne Cocktail,
Three Ways

There's no wrong time for a glass of bubbly, especially if you dress it up with a little something-something. All of these versions are known as brunch drinks, but are just as at home at a nighttime celebration—toasting a big win, a new love, or a gala for a great cause. A big plus for the budget-minded (looking at you, Kip and Fabian) is that the champagne doesn't need to be top shelf when you're adding fruit flavors.

Do yourself and your fellow drinkers a favor and chill the glasses briefly before pouring any of these. Also, always use a flute, not a coupe—a shallower glass lets the celebratory effervescence that is the heart and soul of champagne escape far too quickly. There's a reason why they call it "bubbly"!

Each recipe serves 1

CLASSIC MIMOSA

3 to 4 ounces (90 to 133 ml) chilled champagne

1 to 2 ounces (30 to 60 ml) fresh orange juice

Pour the champagne into a flute so that foam reaches the top. Let it settle and add the orange juice. (A 2 parts champagne to 1 part orange juice ratio is preferred.)

BELLINI

2 ounces (60 ml) peach purée

4 ounces (133 ml) chilled prosecco or sparkling white wine

Mint sprig, optional

Pour the peach purée into a champagne flute, and then slowly add the prosecco so that it foams just enough to mix with purée. Gently stir. Garnish with a mint sprig, if desired.

KIR ROYALE

½ ounce (15 ml) crème de cassis

4 ounces (133 ml) champagne

Lemon twist or raspberry, to garnish, optional

Add the crème de cassis to the bottom of a champagne flute. Slowly pour in the champagne. Garnish with a lemon twist or raspberry, if preferred.

06

DESSERTS TO CHEAT FOR

You don't make it to the top of a brutally competitive sport like hockey, or forge the kind of hard body Ilya, Scott, and other hockey superstars have, without loads and loads of brutal, hard work. Getting there means tons of sacrifice, and denying yourself pleasures today to achieve elusive far-off goals tomorrow. Not a whole lot of sweet in that.

All the deprivation is without any real guarantee that the hard work on the rink, the miles they run, and the weights they lift will actually lead to a championship. Scott, Ilya, Shane, Troy—they've all known the bitter experience of watching as someone else hoists the Cup at center ice on TV. That's gotta leave a bad taste in the mouth.

One sure way to counteract that taste? A sweet indulgence. A simple, sugary extravagance can be miracle medicine, a surefire way to take the sting out of disappointment. And really, what is all the sacrifice for if you can't treat yourself (and those you love) every once in a while?

That's what the wonderful splurges in this chapter are all about: easy, achievable, satisfying decadence. They don't need to be fancy. For instance, the Canadian classic Nanaimo bars on page 129 are a straightforward standard and no less satisfying because of their basic nature. Of course, sometimes what you're after is a special-occasion showstopper. Something like The Tasteful Threesome on page 151 will fill the bill and then some.

Regardless of which you choose, these are meant as meal-enders. Any true dessert is both ending and beginning. They bring the curtain down on the meal and signal that it's just about time to get up from the table and on with your night.

That's the beginning. A dessert can linger on the lips, to be shared with a kiss. The last sweet bit can spark the first sweet bite on the neck or the delicious thrill of pulling his shirt off and running your fingers down those chiseled arms.

So, even if the Cup went to another club, even if it was hoisted by your archrivals, tonight can still be a victory for the home team, and what comes after dessert can be just an extension of the sweetness. Can you say, "Yum-me?"

Num Nanaimo Bars

The allure of some desserts is as much in the memories they hold as in the sugary shades of flavor they contain. Named for an amazingly picturesque city on the coast of Vancouver Island, these bars will be heart-achingly familiar to anyone who grew up there—like Troy Barrett. To people like him, these bring to mind mom, and a taste full of love. The kind of love he hopes one day to have with Harris Drover. All of life should be so sweet. **Makes 16 to 20 bars**

- 1 cup (226 g) plus 2 tablespoons (28 g) unsalted butter, divided and softened
- ¼ cup (49 g) granulated sugar
- 5 tablespoons (40 g) cocoa powder
- 1 large egg, lightly beaten
- 1¾ cups (175 g) graham cracker crumbs
- 1 cup (85 g) sweetened shredded coconut
- 1 teaspoon pure vanilla extract
- Sea salt
- 2 tablespoons (70 g) custard powder
- 2 cups (240 g) confectioners' sugar, sifted
- 2 to 3 tablespoons (30 to 45 ml) heavy whipping cream
- 6 ounces (170 g) semisweet or dark chocolate, coarsely chopped

1. Line an 8 x 8-inch (20 x 20-cm) baking pan with parchment, leaving overhang.
2. To make the base, combine ½ cup (113 g) butter, granulated sugar, and cocoa in a medium heatproof bowl set atop a pot of simmering water, stirring until melted and smooth.
3. Slowly drizzle in the egg, whisking constantly for 1 to 2 minutes, or until the mixture can coat the back of a spoon.
4. Remove from heat and stir in the graham cracker crumbs, coconut, vanilla, and a pinch of salt. Press firmly in an even layer on the bottom of the pan. Refrigerate 30 minutes.
5. Meanwhile, make the filling. In the bowl of a stand mixer fitted with a paddle attachment, beat ½ cup (113 g) butter until pale and fluffy.
6. Beat in the custard powder and confectioners' sugar in ½-cup (60 g) increments, beating between each addition and scraping down sides of the bowl.
7. Beat in the cream and a pinch of salt until smooth. Spread the filling evenly over the chilled base. Refrigerate 30 to 45 minutes, or until firm.
8. Make the topping. Combine the chocolate and the last 2 tablespoons (28 g) butter in a medium heatproof bowl set over a saucepan of simmering water. Stir until melted, smooth, and glossy. Cool for 5 minutes.
9. Evenly spread over the filling. Chill 1 to 2 hours, until fully set.
10. Lift from the baking dish. Cut into bars or squares using a hot, dry knife, wiping between cuts. Refrigerate in an airtight container for up to 1 week.

The Zamboni Celebration

We can't all be pro hockey players. Some of us can't even ice skate backward (for shame!). But we can all aspire to pilot that wonderful behemoth, the Zamboni, between periods. It shaves and levels the ice, providing a glasslike stage for the superstars. This granita-inspired icy dessert takes its cue from that machine and is perfect for humid New York summers or lazy vacations at the cottage. **Serves 6**

- 4 cups (668 g) fresh strawberries, hulled and halved
- ¾ cup (148 g) granulated sugar
- ½ cup (120 ml) water
- 2 teaspoons lemon juice
- 1 teaspoon lemon zest
- ¾ cup (177 g) champagne or sparkling wine
- ¼ cup (60 ml) elderflower liqueur, optional (see note)
- 2 tablespoons (42 g) honey
- 1 teaspoon pure vanilla extract
- Sliced strawberries, for garnish
- Mint, for garnish

Elderflower liqueur is highly recommended for its floral flavor that pairs so well with strawberries. If not using, replace it with additional champagne.

1. In a saucepan over medium heat, combine the strawberries, sugar, and water. Cook for 5 to 7 minutes, stirring occasionally, until the berries soften and release their juices.
2. Remove from heat and stir in the lemon juice and zest. Transfer to a blender and blend on medium-high until completely smooth. (Strain through a fine-mesh sieve into a bowl for a more refined texture.) Set aside to cool.
3. In a small saucepan over low heat, combine the champagne, liqueur (if using), and honey. Cook 2 to 3 minutes, stirring until the honey dissolves. Do not boil. Remove from heat and stir in the vanilla. Set aside to cool completely.
4. Whisk the cooled champagne syrup into the strawberry purée until fully blended. Pour into a 9 x 13-inch (23 x 33-cm) baking dish, and freeze for 1 hour.
5. Use a fork to scrape the frozen edges into the center, and return to the freezer. Repeat every 30 to 40 minutes for 4 hours. The granita is ready when the texture is light, fluffy, and evenly crystallized.
6. Right before serving, fluff the granita one last time. Spoon into chilled coupe glasses or dessert bowls. Garnish with the sliced strawberries and mint. Serve immediately. Freeze, covered, for up to 1 week, fluffing before serving.

Individual Cake Pucks

An actual hockey puck is made of rock-hard vulcanized rubber and is essentially a deadly bullet when flicked off the stick of a sharpshooter center. So, consider the name of this one a small irony. The "cake" in this puck is a delightfully light and airy sponge, and a sinfully delicious icing completes the illusion. (Be sure to use black cocoa for the best effect.) **Makes 12 cakes**

FOR THE CAKES

¾ cup (100 g) all-purpose flour

¼ cup (20 g) black cocoa powder

¾ teaspoon baking soda

½ teaspoon salt

½ cup (99 g) granulated sugar

¼ cup (53 g) packed light brown sugar

1 large egg, room temperature

⅓ cup (80 ml) buttermilk

⅓ cup (80 ml) cooled strong-brewed coffee

¼ cup (60 ml) canola oil

1 teaspoon pure vanilla extract

FOR THE FILLING

1½ cups (360 ml) cold heavy whipping cream

⅓ cup (38 g) confectioners' sugar

1 teaspoon pure vanilla extract

2 tablespoons (28 g) mascarpone

FOR THE GANACHE ICING

6 ounces (170 g) semisweet chocolate, finely chopped

2 tablespoons (64 g) black cocoa powder

¾ cup (180 ml) heavy whipping cream

2 tablespoons (28 g) unsalted butter

2 tablespoons (30 ml) corn syrup or honey

1. Preheat the oven to 350°F (175°C). Add liners to a muffin tin.
2. In a medium bowl, whisk together the flour, cocoa powder, baking soda, and salt.
3. In a large bowl, whisk together sugars, egg, buttermilk, coffee, oil, and vanilla until smooth. Add the dry ingredients; whisk until just combined.
4. Fill the liners halfway (to keep cakes low). Bake 16 to 18 minutes, or until tops are set and a toothpick comes out clean.
5. Cool completely in the pan. Transfer cakes to a wire rack. Trim tops with a serrated knife if domed.
6. To make the filling, follow directions for whipped cream on page 35. Transfer to a piping bag with a 6-mm round tip.
7. Scoop out a shallow cavity in the center of each cupcake. Pipe filling into cavities, slightly mounding. Chill for 20 minutes to firm up.
8. Meanwhile, make the ganache. In a medium heatproof bowl, combine chocolate and cocoa.
9. In a saucepan over medium heat, warm cream and butter until just simmering. Pour over chocolate. Let sit for 1 minute; stir until smooth and glossy. Stir in corn syrup or honey. Cool until thickened but still pourable.
10. Arrange cupcakes on a wire rack set over a tray lined with parchment paper. Spoon ganache over each cupcake, allowing it to flow evenly to the edges. Use an offset spatula if needed.
11. Refrigerate 30 to 45 minutes to set, and for up to 3 days. Bring to room temperature before serving.

Home Rink Blueberry-Apple Slump

Nobody wants the kind of slump that Scott Hunter was in when he happened into the smoothie shop. But his experience is proof positive that any slump is just one smoothie away from becoming a winning streak, and this dessert is proof positive that not all slumps are a bad thing. In fact, this particularly homey dessert includes two fruits—Kip's favorite blueberries and Harris Drover's apples—that prove no matter how bad things get, the love of your life may be just over the horizon or around the next corner. **Serves 6**

FOR THE BASE

4 cups (544 g) fresh or frozen blueberries

2 medium apples, peeled, cored, and cut into ½-inch (12-mm) cubes

¾ cup (148 g) granulated sugar

1 tablespoon (15 ml) lemon juice

1 teaspoon pure vanilla extract

½ teaspoon apple pie spice

Pinch sea salt

⅓ cup (80 ml) water

FOR THE DUMPLINGS

1½ cups (200 g) all-purpose flour

2 tablespoons (25 g) granulated sugar

2 teaspoons baking powder

½ teaspoon kosher salt

¼ cup (57 g) cold unsalted butter, cubed

¾ cup (180 ml) whole milk or buttermilk

FOR THE SYRUP

¾ cup (180 ml) dark rum

½ cup (118 ml) pure maple syrup

2 tablespoons (28 g) unsalted butter

Pinch sea salt

MAKE THE BASE

1. In a large, heavy saucepan or deep skillet, combine the ingredients. Bring to a gentle simmer over medium heat.
2. Cook for 12 to 15 minutes, stirring occasionally, until apples are tender. The mixture should be syrupy but chunky. Reduce heat to low and keep warm.

MAKE THE DUMPLINGS

1. In a large bowl, whisk together the dry ingredients. Cut in cold butter using a pastry cutter or your fingers, until the mixture resembles coarse crumbs.
2. Add milk or buttermilk and mix just until a soft dough forms. Dough should be tender and slightly sticky.
3. Drop heaping tablespoons of dough directly into warm blueberry-apple mixture, leaving space between dumplings.
4. Cover and reduce heat to low. Steam dumplings for 18 to 22 minutes. They're done when puffed and cooked through. (Try not to lift the lid while cooking.)

MAKE THE SYRUP

1. In a small saucepan over medium heat, combine the ingredients. Bring to a gentle simmer for 6 to 8 minutes, or until slightly thickened and glossy.
2. Spoon warm slump and dumplings into shallow bowls. Drizzle generously with syrup and serve.

Heart Hands Russian Tea Cakes

The world may be oblivious to Shane and Ilya's true connection, even years after they started their joint charity, but it doesn't take long for the daughters of Shane's teammate Hayden to get wise. Eventually, the girls even ask the two hockey superstars if they are each other's husbands. These cookies are tribute to the Russian half of the wedding that should be, and the adorable little girls who know. Not coincidentally, the other name for these treats is "wedding cookies." **Makes 36 to 40 cookies**

- 1 cup (112 g) walnut halves
- 1 cup (114 g) chopped pecans
- 1 cup (226 g) unsalted butter, softened
- 2¼ cups (254 g) confectioners' sugar, divided
- 2 teaspoons pure vanilla extract
- ½ teaspoon almond extract
- 2¼ cups (270 g) all-purpose flour
- 2 tablespoons (16 g) cornstarch
- ½ teaspoon sea salt
- 4 teaspoons (or 1 packet [8 g]) vanilla sugar, optional

1. Preheat the oven to 350°F (175°C). Line a baking sheet with parchment paper.
2. Spread nuts on the baking sheet, keeping separate. Toast 6 to 8 minutes, until fragrant.
3. Let cool completely, then grind the walnuts finely.
4. In the bowl of stand mixer fitted with a paddle attachment, cream the butter and ¾ cup (90 g) confectioners' sugar until pale and fluffy, 2 to 3 minutes. Add the extracts; beat until combined.
5. In a medium bowl, whisk together flour, cornstarch, and salt. Gradually add to butter mixture, while mixing on low.
6. Fold in the nuts until evenly distributed. Dough should be soft, but not sticky. Cover and refrigerate 45 minutes.
7. Reduce oven temperature to 325°F (165°C). Line 2 baking sheets with parchment paper.
8. Scoop tablespoon-sized mounds of cookie dough and roll into smooth balls. Space them 1½ inches (4 cm) apart on the baking sheets.
9. Bake for 18 to 22 minutes, or until set and pale golden on the bottoms. Tops should still be pale, not browned.
10. Cool cookies for 5 minutes on the tray. While still warm, roll gently in the remaining 1½ cups (164 g) confectioners' sugar. Set on a wire rack to cool completely.
11. Once fully cooled, roll cookies again in confectioners' sugar, mixed with the vanilla sugar, if using. Serve immediately or store in an airtight container for up to 1 week.

It Is What It's-It

Only in the *Heated Rivalry* universe does the San Francisco Mission hockey team exist, but the City by the Bay has a special dessert called *It's-It*—vanilla ice cream sandwiched between two oatmeal cookies and dipped in chocolate. This unique cold treat is a nod to the fictional team and to the real-life ice cream treat offered in the actual Bay Area. **Makes 8 sandwich cookies**

- 1 cup (226 g) unsalted butter, softened
- 1 cup (213 g) packed light brown sugar
- ½ cup (99 g) granulated sugar
- 2 large eggs, room temperature
- 2 teaspoons pure vanilla extract
- 1½ cups (200 g) all-purpose flour
- 1 teaspoon baking soda
- 1 teaspoon ground cinnamon
- ½ teaspoon fine sea salt
- 3 cups (240 g) old-fashioned oats
- 1 quart (946 ml) premium vanilla ice cream, slightly softened
- 12 ounces (340 g) semisweet or dark chocolate, chopped
- 2 tablespoons (30 ml) coconut oil

1. Preheat oven to 350°F (175°C). Line 2 baking sheets with parchment paper.
2. In the bowl of stand mixer fitted with a paddle attachment, cream the butter and sugars until light and fluffy, 2 to 3 minutes.
3. Add eggs one at a time, mixing well after each addition. Add the vanilla.
4. In a medium bowl, whisk together flour, baking soda, cinnamon, and salt. Slowly add to the wet mixture; mix just until incorporated. Fold in oats.
5. Scoop ¼-cup (80 g) dough mounds onto baking sheets, spacing 2 inches (5 cm) apart. Flatten slightly. Bake 10 to 12 minutes, or until edges are golden but centers still soft. Transfer to wire racks to cool completely.
6. Line a baking pan with parchment paper. Spread the ice cream in the pan, in an even ¾-inch-thick (2-cm) layer. Freeze 1 to 2 hours, until firm enough to cut.
7. Use a round cutter slightly smaller than cookies to cut discs out of the ice cream. Sandwich discs between the flat sides of 2 cookies. Press firmly but gently to seal. Transfer to a parchment-lined baking sheet and freeze for 1 hour or until firm.
8. Meanwhile, in a medium heatproof bowl set over a pot of simmering water, combine the chocolate and coconut oil. Stir until smooth and glossy.
9. Let cool so the chocolate it is still warm and fluid, but not hot (ideally 88°F to 92°F [31°C to 33°C]).
10. Holding a sandwich cookie with 2 forks, dip completely into chocolate. Or spoon chocolate over each cookie while holding over the bowl.
11. Set coated cookies on the tray. Freeze 20 to 30 minutes or until chocolate is firm. Wrap sandwiches and freeze in an airtight container for up to 2 weeks. Rest at room temperature 5 minutes before serving.

Off-Season Summer Berry Pavlova

Summer is when hockey superstars turn into ordinary vacationers. They can dangle their feet in the lake outside their back door (looking at you, Shane and Ilya) or take an aimless window-shopping stroll through the humid streets of SoHo (eyes on you, Eric and Kyle). No matter where they are, summer dinners call for a light-as-air dessert like this one. **Serves 8**

6 large egg whites, room temperature

Pinch sea salt

1½ cups (285 g) superfine sugar

2 teaspoons cornstarch

1 teaspoon white vinegar

2 teaspoons pure vanilla extract, divided

1 cup (167 g) sliced fresh strawberries

1 cup (120 g) fresh raspberries

1 cup (140 g) fresh blueberries

1 cup (120 g) fresh blackberries

3 tablespoons (37 g) granulated sugar

1 tablespoon (15 ml) lemon juice

1½ cups (356 ml) very cold heavy whipping cream

3 tablespoons (24 g) confectioners' sugar

Fresh berries, mint leaves, and confectioners' sugar, for serving

1. Preheat the oven to 250°F (120°C). Line a baking sheet with parchment paper. Draw a 9-inch (23-cm) circle in pencil as a guide, and flip the parchment.
2. In the bowl of stand mixer fitted with a whisk attachment beat the egg whites and salt on medium until soft peaks form.
3. Slowly add superfine sugar, 1 tablespoon (12 g) at a time, beating well after each addition. Continue beating until meringue is thick, glossy, and holds stiff peaks. Rub a bit of meringue between your fingers; it should feel smooth, not gritty.
4. Sprinkle in the cornstarch, vinegar, and 1 teaspoon vanilla. Fold in gently without deflating the meringue.
5. Spoon meringue onto the parchment circle and shape into a level round. Create a slight well in the center.
6. Place in oven and immediately reduce temperature to 225°F (105°C). Bake for 90 minutes, or until exterior is crisp and dry.
7. Turn oven off, crack door slightly (wedge a wooden spoon in the door), and let pavlova cool completely, at least 2 hours.
8. In a large bowl, combine the berries, granulated sugar, and lemon juice. Toss gently; let sit for 20 to 30 minutes, or until berries release juices and become glossy. Refrigerate.
9. In a large, chilled bowl, use a hand mixer to whip the heavy cream, confectioners' sugar, and 1 teaspoon vanilla until soft peaks form. The mixture should be creamy but billowy.
10. Carefully transfer the cooled pavlova to a serving platter. Spoon cream into the center well, spreading it slightly but keeping height.
11. Spoon berries generously over the cream, allowing juices to cascade down the sides. Garnish with berries and mint, and dust lightly with confectioners' sugar just before serving.

The Montreal Brownies

Whether you think of them as the Metros or the Voyageurs, Montreal is ever the rival of Boston, as is dark-haired Shane to blonde Ilya. But even as they battle, even as we take in the particular charms of one side or another, we need to remember the sweetness that lies between, the hidden affection that bubbles beneath the surface. The same is true of these brownies and the blondie recipe that follows. They are the light and dark sides to the same ooey, gooey, sweet-and-chewy coin. Opposites never tasted so good, and you'll have a hard time choosing. **Makes 12 to 16 brownies**

¾ cup (170 g) unsalted butter, plus more for greasing

10 ounces (283 g) high-quality dark chocolate (70% to 75% cocoa), coarsely chopped

1¼ cups (247 g) granulated sugar

½ cup (106 g) packed dark brown sugar

3 large eggs, room temperature

2 teaspoons pure vanilla extract

5 tablespoons (75 ml) bourbon, divided

¾ cup (100 g) all-purpose flour

¼ cup (20 g) Dutch-process cocoa powder

½ teaspoon sea salt

¾ cup (133 g) dark chocolate chips

½ cup (120 ml) pure maple syrup

3 ounces (85 g) dark chocolate, finely chopped

2 tablespoons (30 ml) heavy whipping cream

Confectioners' sugar, for dusting

1. Preheat the oven to 350°F (175°C). Line a 9 x 9-inch (23 x 23-cm) baking pan with parchment, leaving overhang. Lightly butter the parchment.
2. In a medium heatproof bowl set over a pot of gently simmering water, combine the coarsely chopped dark chocolate and butter. Stir until smooth. Let cool slightly.
3. Whisk in the sugars until completely incorporated. Add eggs, one at a time, whisking until glossy and thick after each addition. Stir in vanilla and 3 tablespoons (45 ml) bourbon.
4. In a separate medium bowl, whisk together flour, cocoa powder, and salt. Fold into the batter until just combined. Fold in the chocolate chips. Transfer to the pan and smooth the top.
5. In a small saucepan, combine the maple syrup and 2 tablespoons (30 ml) bourbon over low heat and warm for 2 to 3 minutes. Add finely chopped chocolate and cream. Stir until melted and glossy. Let cool slightly until it is thick but still pourable.
6. Spoon over brownie base, and use a knife to create gentle swirls.
7. Bake 30 to 35 minutes, or until edges are set and center is slightly soft. Do not overbake; texture is meant to be gooey.
8. Cool brownies completely in the pan. Lift brownies out; cut into squares using a hot knife, wiping the blade between cuts. Dust generously with confectioners' sugar. Store, covered, at room temperature, for up to 5 days.

B

The Boston Blondies

Just as Ilya is Boston's wisecracking, bawdy yang to Montreal's conservative, button-down Shane's yin, this addictive sweet is the butterscotch alternative to the chocolaty enticements of The Montreal Brownies (page 143). Brown butter gives this creation a distinctively nutty essence that adds richness to the otherwise dominant sweetness. Fortunately, just as Ilya and Shane share an overarching love, this dessert shares an incredible gooey mouth feel with its brownie counterpart. Go team! **Makes 12 to 16 blondies**

- 1 cup (226 g) unsalted butter
- 1½ cups (320 g) packed light brown sugar
- ½ cup (99 g) granulated sugar
- 2 large eggs, room temperature
- 2½ teaspoons pure vanilla extract, divided
- 2 cups (240 g) all-purpose flour
- 1 teaspoon baking powder
- ¾ teaspoon sea salt
- 1½ cups (171 g) pecans, coarsely chopped and toasted
- 1½ cups (170 g) confectioners' sugar, sifted
- 2 to 3 tablespoons (30 to 45 ml) heavy whipping cream or whole milk

1. Preheat oven to 350°F (175°C). Line a 9 x 13-inch (23 x 33-cm) baking dish with parchment paper, leaving overhang.
2. In a medium saucepan over medium heat, melt butter, swirling frequently. Cook until it turns deep golden brown and smells nutty, about 7 minutes.
3. Remove from heat and pour into a heatproof bowl, scraping up the browned bits. Cool for 10 to 15 minutes, until still warm but not hot.
4. Whisk sugars into the cooled brown butter. Add eggs, whisking until glossy and emulsified. Stir in 2 teaspoons vanilla.
5. In a medium bowl, whisk together flour, baking powder, and salt. Fold into the butter mixture until just combined. Fold in the pecans.
6. Spread batter evenly in the pan. Bake 25 to 30 minutes, or until edges are golden and center is just set. A toothpick stuck in the center should come out with a few moist crumbs on it, but not wet. Cool completely in the pan.
7. In a small bowl, whisk together confectioners' sugar, 2 tablespoons (30 ml) cream or milk, and ½ teaspoon vanilla until smooth and pourable. Add more cream or milk as necessary to adjust the consistency. Pour over blondies and spread evenly with an offset spatula. Let set for 20 to 30 minutes.
8. Lift the blondies from the pan and cut into squares. Serve at room temperature for the softest texture. Store, covered, at room temperature for up to 5 days.

Pouding Chômeur

Ilya may act perturbed the first time he hears Shane give an interview in perfect Quebecois French, but he's also clearly impressed. Why wouldn't he be? Everything sounds a little fancier in French and that includes this dessert, the name for which translates to "Poor Man's Pudding." But there's nothing poor about the layers of flavor and textures captured in cakelike dumplings swimming in a dark amber sauce. One taste and you'll realize that French is the language of *amour*. **Serves 8**

FOR THE SAUCE

2 cups (472 ml) pure dark maple syrup

1 cup (240 ml) heavy whipping cream

½ cup (120 ml) whole milk

½ packed cup (106 g) brown sugar

3 tablespoons (42 g) unsalted butter

1 teaspoon pure vanilla extract

Pinch sea salt

FOR THE DUMPLINGS

1½ cups (200 g) all-purpose flour

2 teaspoons baking powder

½ teaspoon sea salt

¼ teaspoon baking soda

½ cup (113 g) unsalted butter, softened, plus more for the dish

¾ cup (148 g) granulated sugar

2 large eggs, room temperature

1 teaspoon pure vanilla extract

½ cup (120 ml) whole milk

¼ cup (60 ml) heavy whipping cream or crème fraîche

MAKE THE SAUCE

1. In a medium saucepan over medium heat, combine maple syrup, cream, milk, and brown sugar. Bring to a simmer, stirring until sugar dissolves, about 3 minutes.
2. Add butter and cook 2 to 3 minutes, until the butter is melted and sauce is thickened slightly.
3. Remove from heat and stir in vanilla and salt. Keep warm over lowest heat setting.

MAKE THE DUMPLINGS

1. Preheat the oven to 350°F (175°C). Grease a 9 x 13-inch (23 x 33-cm) baking dish or deep gratin dish.
2. In a medium bowl, whisk together the dry ingredients.
3. In the bowl of stand mixer fitted with a paddle attachment, cream butter and sugar until pale and fluffy, about 4 minutes.
4. Add eggs one at a time, beating until incorporated. Add vanilla and mix until incorporated.
5. Add dry ingredients in 2 batches, alternating with milk and cream. Mix until just combined. Batter should be thick, smooth, and spoonable.
6. Pour warm sauce into the baking dish. Drop in dumpling batter by large spoonfuls. Don't spread; the batter will expand as it bakes.
7. Bake 40 to 45 minutes, or until dumplings are golden brown, centers are set but tender, and sauce is bubbling around edges.
8. Let rest 10 to 15 minutes. Sauce will thicken slightly. Spoon dumplings into shallow bowls and ladle sauce generously over top. Serve warm.

PUCK IT!
0

Oh Canada, Butter Bars

As Ilya settles in to play for the Ottawa Centaurs, he'd better learn to love this classic—inspired by the butter tart that can rightfully be called the Canadian national dessert. But because the heroes of the Game Changers series are more drawn to bars (and, occasionally, night clubs), we've transformed the classic tarts into these super-rich bars. Be warned, they're as addictive as the series itself! **Makes 16 bars**

2 cups (240 g) plus 1 tablespoon (8 g) all-purpose flour, divided

½ cup (99 g) granulated sugar

½ teaspoon sea salt, divided

1 cup (226 g) cold unsalted butter, cubed

2 teaspoons pure vanilla extract, divided

¾ cup (112 g) raisins

Boiling water

1 cup (240 ml) pure maple syrup

¾ packed cup (159 g) dark brown sugar

½ cup (113 g) unsalted butter, melted and cooled slightly

3 large eggs, room temperature

2 tablespoons (30 ml) heavy cream

1 tablespoon (15 ml) apple cider vinegar

1. Preheat the oven to 350°F (175°C). Line a 9 x 13-inch (23 x 33-cm) baking pan with parchment, leaving overhang.
2. Make the shortbread: In a large bowl, whisk together 2 cups (240 g) flour, the granulated sugar, and ¼ teaspoon salt. Cut in the cold cubed butter using a pastry cutter or your fingers until the mixture resembles coarse crumbs.
3. Stir in 1 teaspoon vanilla and gently bring the dough together. Press evenly into the pan, pressing it into the corners and leveling it out. Use a fork to prick the surface all over.
4. Bake for 18 to 20 minutes, or until light golden brown at the edges. Let cool in the pan on a wire rack while you prepare the filling. Reduce oven temperature to 325°F (165°C).
5. Make the filling: In a small bowl, cover the raisins with boiling water and let soak for 20 minutes. Drain and pat the raisins dry with paper towels.
6. In a large bowl, whisk together the maple syrup and brown sugar until smooth. Whisk in 1 tablespoon (8 g) flour until no lumps remain.
7. Slowly stream in the melted butter, whisking continuously. Add the eggs one at a time, whisking until fully incorporated but not frothy.
8. Stir in the heavy cream, vinegar, 1 teaspoon vanilla, and ¼ teaspoon salt until glossy and fully emulsified.
9. Sprinkle the raisins evenly over the shortbread crust. Pour the filling gently over top, carefully spreading evenly to the edges. Tap the pan lightly on the counter to release air bubbles.
10. Bake 25 to 30 minutes, or until the filling is set at the edges but slightly soft in the center. The surface should appear glossy with light caramelization.
11. Cool completely in the pan. Refrigerate for 2 hours to fully set the filling for a classic butter tart texture.
12. Lift from the pan and slice into 16 bars with a hot, dry knife, cleaning the blade between cuts. Serve at room temperature or slightly chilled. Refrigerate bars, sealed, for up to 1 week.

The Tasteful Threesome

Spoiler alert ahead! But honestly? You don't have to have read the books to know (or at least hope) that Ilya and Shane get their happily ever after. Though it happens sooner than Shane's original multiyear plan, the couple finally get to publicly declare their love. And despite this dessert's cheeky name, they will only ever have eyes for each other. **Serves 12**

FOR THE BASE

½ cup (60 g) all-purpose flour

¼ cup (20 g) cocoa powder

¼ teaspoon fine sea salt

6 ounces (170 g) dark chocolate, chopped

½ cup (113 g) unsalted butter

¾ cup (148 g) granulated sugar

3 large eggs, room temperature

1 teaspoon pure vanilla extract

FOR THE MOUSSE

7 ounces (196 g) dark chocolate (70% cocoa), chopped

6 cups (1.42 L) heavy whipping cream, divided

3½ tablespoons (53 g) confectioners' sugar, divided

2 teaspoons pure vanilla extract, divided

Sea salt

7 ounces (196 g) milk chocolate, chopped

7 ounces (196 g) white chocolate, chopped

FOR THE GLAZE

6 ounces (170 g) semisweet chocolate, chopped

¾ cup (180 ml) heavy cream

1 tablespoon (14 g) unsalted butter

Chocolate curls, white chocolate shards, cocoa powder, or fresh berries, for garnish

(Recipe continues on next page)

MAKE THE BASE

1. Preheat oven to 350°F (175°C). Line the bottom of a 9-inch (23-cm) springform pan with parchment paper.
2. Sift together the flour, cocoa powder, and salt into a medium bowl.
3. In a medium heatproof bowl placed over a pot of simmering water, combine the chocolate and butter, stirring until melted and smooth. Whisk in the sugar until dissolved.
4. Add the eggs one at a time, whisking until the mixture is glossy. Stir in the vanilla until incorporated.
5. Gently fold the dry ingredients into the wet until just combined.
6. Pour the batter into the pan. Bake 18 to 22 minutes, or until just set. The center of the cake should spring back lightly when touched. Place on a wire rack and cool completely in the pan.

MAKE THE MOUSSE

1. Make the dark chocolate mousse by placing the dark chocolate in a large heatproof bowl.
2. In a small saucepan over low heat, heat ¾ cup (180 ml) of the cream just until simmering. Pour over the chocolate and let sit for 1 minute, then stir until completely smooth. Let cool to room temperature, but it should still be runny.
3. In the bowl of stand mixer fitted with a whisk attachment, combine 1¼ cups (300 ml) cream, 2 tablespoons (16 g) confectioners' sugar, 1 teaspoon vanilla, and a pinch of salt. Whip to soft peaks.
4. Fold the whipped cream into the melted chocolate in three additions until it's a uniform, light, and airy texture.
5. Spoon the mousse onto the cake base and smooth it level. Chill for 45 to 60 minutes, until lightly set.
6. Make the milk chocolate mousse using the same process, but 1½ tablespoons (12 g) sugar and ½ teaspoon vanilla. Spread the milk chocolate mousse over the dark chocolate mousse and chill until set.
7. Make the white chocolate mousse using the same process, but omitting the sugar and using only ½ teaspoon vanilla. Spread the white chocolate mousse over the milk chocolate mousse and chill until set.

GLAZE THE CAKE

1. Place the chocolate in a large heatproof bowl.
2. In a small saucepan over low heat, heat the cream just until simmering. Pour over the chocolate and let sit for 1 minute. Stir until glossy. Stir in the butter until completely incorporated. Cool until just warm, but still pourable.
3. Remove the cake from the pan and place on a wire rack set over a baking tray lined with parchment paper. Slowly pour the glaze over top, allowing it to drip down the sides. Smooth the surface, if desired, and chill for 30 minutes to set the glaze.
4. To serve, slice the cake with a hot, dry knife, wiping it clean between slices. Garnish with chocolate curls, white chocolate shards, a dusting of cocoa, or fresh berries, as you prefer. Refrigerate, covered, for up to 4 days.

OVERTIME: AWARDS BANQUET MENUS

The right dish makes the meal, but a thoughtful combination of dishes makes an extraordinary occasion. Creating a menu that celebrates and elevates a special day or a particular moment in time is a little bit like creating a championship hockey team. You start by combining powerful performers that are standouts in their own right and that complement one another—making sure none overshadows the others. You know where to put a Scott Hunter so that he performs his best (wink, wink, nudge, nudge, Kip), and how to optimize Ryan Price's specific talents to the benefit of the whole team. When everything comes together perfectly, it becomes a uniquely memorable centerpiece to share with the people that matter most to you. And that's really what these menus are all about.

A Perfect Valentine's Dinner

Sure—chocolates, flowers, and champagne are all well and lovely. But if you really want to knock the socks (and all the other clothing) off that special someone, put the effort in and create a one-of-kind romantic meal. Food is the ultimate love language and, let's not forget, it is literally the caloric fuel for physical passion.

- First Valentine's Salad 41
- Steak au Frites for Two 91
- Mock Mule for Winners 109
- Or Kir Royale 125
- Heart Hands Russian Tea Cakes 137

Game-Day Watch Party Spread

Fandom is just another form of love. When you choose sides in an athletic contest, you're marrying into a fraternity. You put on your face paint and claim the team as your own. You scream your head off as you watch the goals and body checks. It's a connection through ritual, a ritual that includes perfect foods for your collective spirit. Go team!

- Grind(him) Grinder 51
- Ultimate Bar Fries 61
- Airport Lounge Trail Mix 59
- All-Star Game Mango Salsa and Homemade Pita Chips 69
- Game-Day Dip, Three Ways 71
- Crockpot Mulled Cider 107
- Num Nanaimo Bars 129

Dudelicious Dinner Party

This one's for the boys. Every once in a while you need to gather the homeboys for some good old-fashioned bonding. (It's okay if that includes a little flirting.) The point is to connect and cement those friendships, clock in some bro time, and have some fun. The right chow is crucial, not only to feeding your hungry buds, but for setting the mood. (Don't forget the beers!)

- Chicken Salad for Contenders 45
- Steak-a-Bobs for Sharing 77
- Airport Lounge Trail Mix 59
- Light Up the Net 123
- The Montreal Brownies or Boston Blondies 143–145

Summer Vacay Brunch

Mmm . . . warm days, sunny mornings, no work (or practice), and pure laziness. Funny how all that can build up an appetite. Coincidentally, those are the perfect circumstances for brunch: A meal not so early that you have to get up on schedule, and not so late that it's legitimately midday. Embrace the meal that appeals to off-season hockey stars as they soak up the vitamin D their bodies have been craving all winter.

- Easy Weekend Blinis 17
- New York–Style Bagel and Lox 29
- Slapshot Biscuits 65
- A Quiche Before You Go 87
- Champagne Cocktail, Three Ways 125
- Flirty Blueberry Smoothie 111
- Off-Season Summer Berry Pavlova 141

Warm Night Cottage Dinner

There are certain long, star-filled nights that you just want to go on forever. That lovely time after a busy, sunny day where you just want to sit by a cozy fire and maybe listen for loons (or other creatures). Your meal has to be easy to make, and it helps if your drink doubles as dessert. Don't bother cleaning up the dishes; just see where the warm night takes you . . .

- Off-the-Ice Summer Pasta Salad 39
- Big W Grilled Pork Chops with Pesto 99
- Northern Lights Julep 119

An Intimate Tryst Platter

Just as this cookbook takes its inspiration from hockey and passion, this menu takes its inspiration from the casual dining experience of tapas and the Spanish love of good food and long nights. It's true that you might not come across many Spanish hockey players, but that shouldn't stop you from eating like it's date night on the Costa del Sol. After all, before he met Kip, Scott Hunter spent his off-season vacations taking in the local delectables. It doesn't have to be love; sometimes a simple tryst can satisfy your hunger.

- Penthouse Room-Service Caesar Salad 43
- Date Night Chicken Marsala 103
- Maple-Roasted Carrots for Two 63
- *Pouding Chômeur* 147
- The Canadian Hat Trick 121

MVP Celebration Cocktail Party

Might be a graduation. Maybe it's a new job. Perhaps a promotion, or any other positive life-changing event. Life's best moments are meant to be celebrated, and this meal puts the spotlight on the big achiever. The focus here is on the chillier circumstances of a winter hockey championship and the MVP ceremony that follows. Because, after all, Scott, Ilya, and Shane have all hoisted that trophy. Which is to say, they have all feasted on the fruits of their labors. Thankfully, you don't need to win an MVP award to eat like one.

- The Waiter's-Crash Canapés 67
- Chicken Salad for Contenders 45
- MVP Sheet-Pan Thighs to Die For 81
- Rookie of the Year 113
- Home Rink Blueberry-Apple Slump 135
- The Zamboni Celebration 131

INDEX

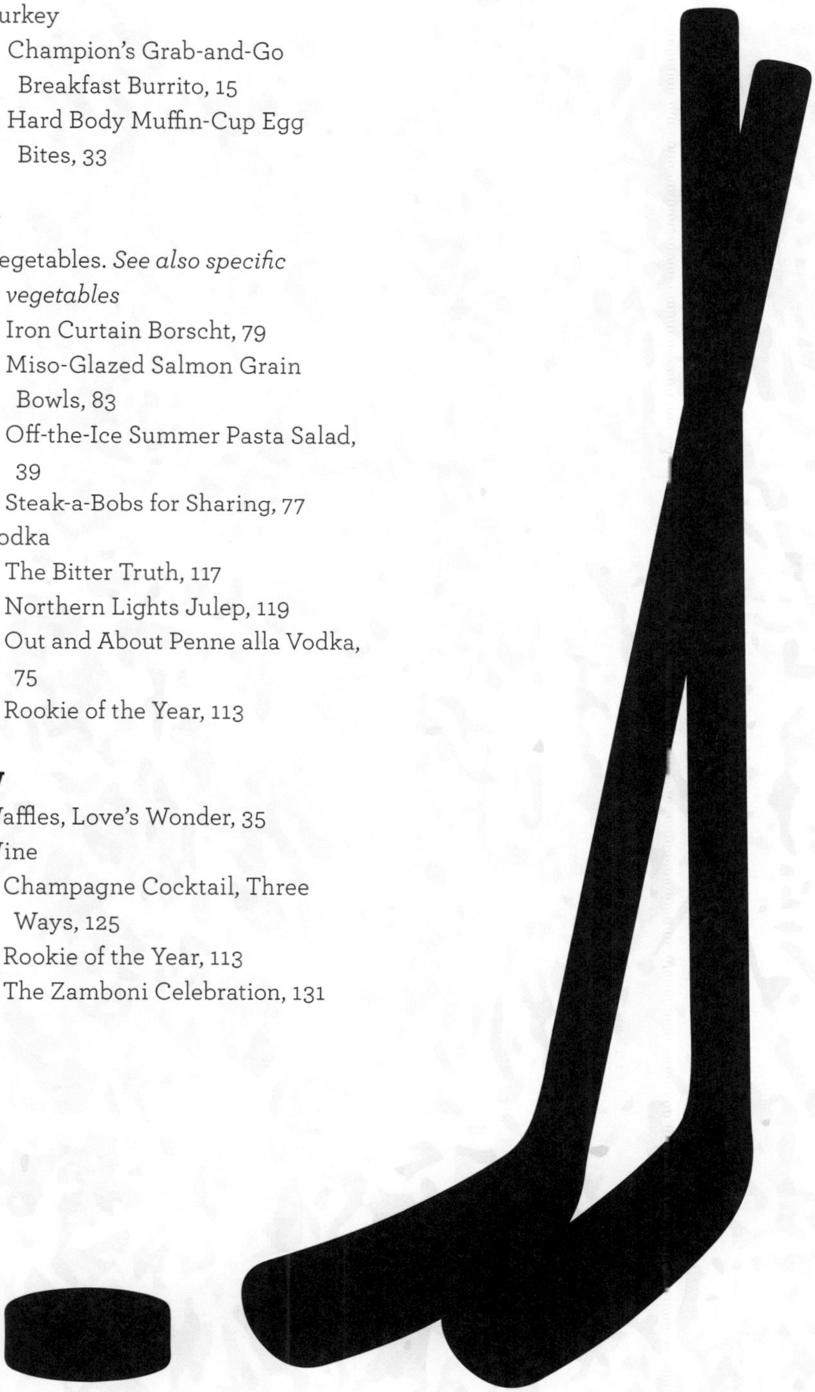

LOVE
IS LOVE
IS LOVE

FIELD TRIPS

MUSEUMS

Heather Kissock

AV2

www.av2books.com

Step 1
Go to **www.av2books.com**

Step 2
Enter this unique code
IUNELBPD2

Step 3
Explore your interactive eBook!

AV2 is optimized for use on any device

Your interactive eBook comes with...

Contents
Browse a live contents page to easily navigate through resources

Audio
Listen to sections of the book read aloud

Videos
Watch informative video clips

Weblinks
Gain additional information for research

Try This!
Complete activities and hands-on experiments

Key Words
Study vocabulary, and complete a matching word activity

Quizzes
Test your knowledge

Slideshows
View images and captions

... and much, much more!

FIELD TRIPS

MUSEUMS

Contents

Why Visit a Museum?

Visiting a museum is a way to learn about the past. Museums are places where people can see objects from long ago. Some museums show how people lived in the past. Other museums have paintings and **sculptures** on display. People can even visit a museum to see what types of animals once roamed Earth.

Museums are important places. They help people understand what life was like many years ago. They also show how the world has changed over time.

Many museums allow visitors to interact with the items on display. This gives them a hands-on learning experience.

More than 1 billion objects are kept in U.S. museums alone.

The United States has more than **35,000 museums.**

U.S. museums receive about **850 million visits** per year.

Museum Hopping

Most museums have a special area of focus. Their **collections** may be devoted to an ancient people or modern technology. Some museums explore one subject in detail. Car museums, for example, can be found in countries around the world.

There are six main types of museum. All museums can be placed in one of these categories.

History Museums

These museums focus on the history of a place and its people. They contain objects from early times and show how the place or people developed over time.

Natural History Museums

Natural history museums display objects found in nature. These objects may be from the past or the present. People can go to these museums to see dinosaur **fossils** or to look at gemstones and other rocks.

Science and Technology Museums

Science and technology museums help people understand how science works. They often display scientific inventions and show how they came to be.

General Museums

General museums cover a wide range of topics. They allow people to explore history, art, and science all in one place. These museums often show the local history and characteristics of a region or town.

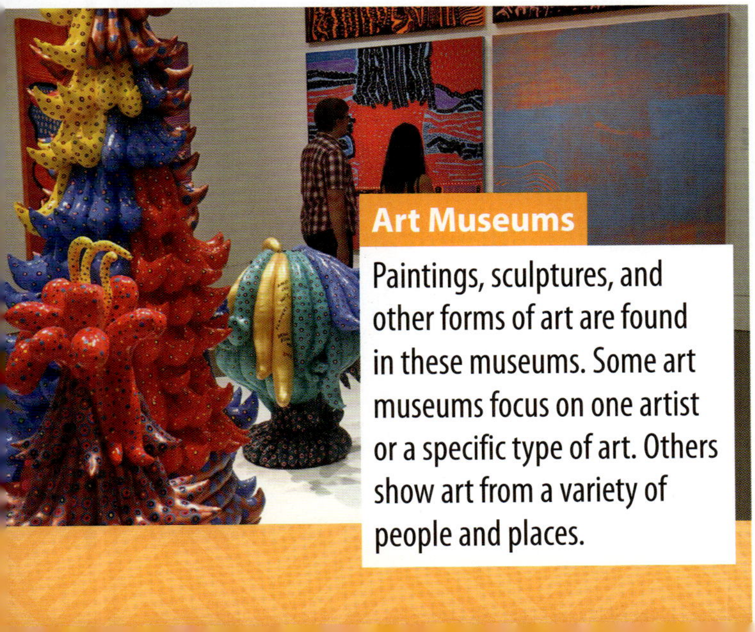

Art Museums

Paintings, sculptures, and other forms of art are found in these museums. Some art museums focus on one artist or a specific type of art. Others show art from a variety of people and places.

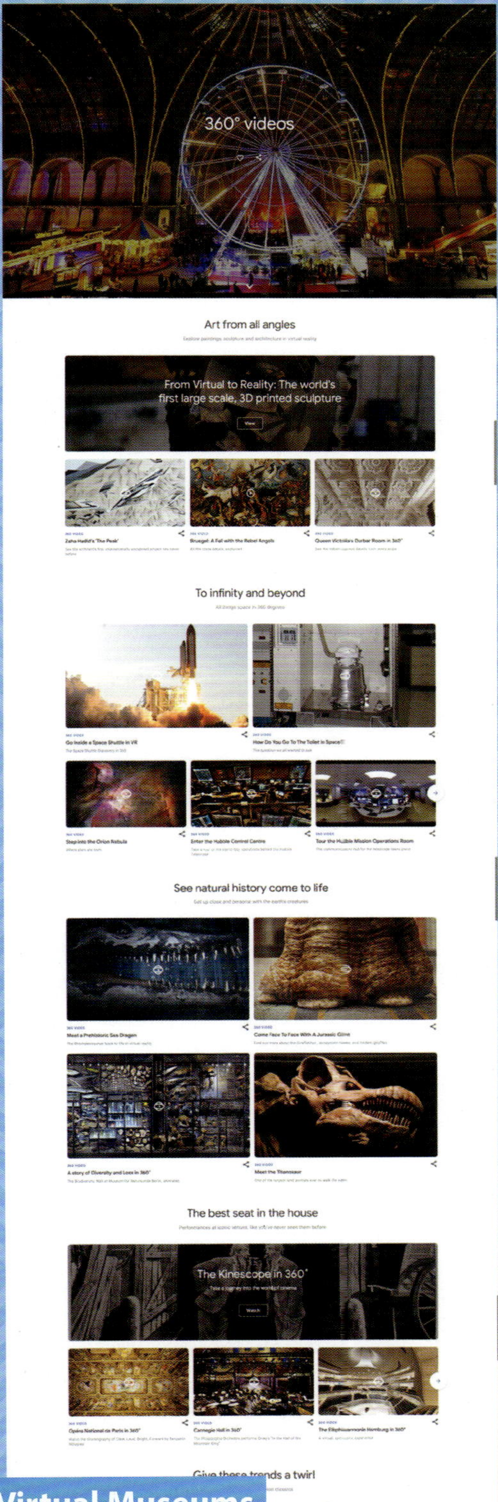

Virtual Museums

This type of museum is only found online. Most virtual museums are linked to other museums. They contain pictures of the objects a museum has in its collection.

Museums around the World

Museums can be found in most countries. Some are known around the world. Others are important to the area in which they reside.

1

Smithsonian National Museum of Natural History
Washington, United States

This museum covers an area larger than 18 football fields. It holds the world's largest collection of natural history **artifacts**.

2

Musée du Louvre
Paris, France

The Musée du Louvre is the largest art museum in the world. It is home to more than 460,000 artworks and artifacts.

3

Shanghai Science and Technology Museum   Shanghai, China

This science museum has 14 exhibit halls and 4 IMAX theaters. Its theaters hold more than 10,000 science movie screenings every year.

4

Museum of Egyptian Antiquities Cairo, Egypt

More than 120,000 artifacts from ancient Egypt are housed within this museum. Visitors can see mummies, pottery, and jewelry from thousands of years ago.

5

São Paulo Museum of Art São Paulo, Brazil

Founded in 1947, this was Brazil's first modern art museum. Today, it is home to more than 10,000 pieces of art.

6

Australian War Memorial Canberra, Australia

Opened in 1941, this memorial's museum tells the story of Australia at war. In 2016, it was voted the country's top landmark.

Lighting

Light plays an important role in a gallery. It highlights the works and shows them at their best.

Partitions

Partitions are small walls within a gallery. They allow more works to be displayed and also help guide visitors through the space.

Display Cases

Smaller pieces are sometimes given their own display space. Visitors can walk around these works and view them from all sides.

Seating

Most galleries have seating. It encourages visitors to relax and spend time reflecting on the works around them.

Galleries

Museums are made up of a series of rooms. These rooms are called galleries. A gallery can be large or small. Its size depends on the objects being displayed.

Galleries contain objects that share something in common. A gallery in an art museum might contain paintings from the 1800s. A history museum could have a gallery devoted to farming tools. These objects may be hung on a wall or put in display cases.

To make an exhibit even more exciting, a museum may hang artifacts from the ceiling of its galleries.

What to See in a Museum

Visiting a museum can feel like a trip to another world. The objects found there can be quite unfamiliar to people today. Museums try to display objects in ways that allow people to understand them better.

Carnegie Museum of Natural History

At Pennsylvania's Carnegie Museum of Natural History, people walk through a prehistoric world to look at dinosaur fossils. They see what types of plants and animals made up each dinosaur's **habitat**.

West of the Pecos Museum

Visitors to Texas's West of the Pecos Museum stand in a kitchen to view the cooking tools **pioneers** used long ago. They get a feel for the amount of work it took to make a meal back then.

Ontario Science Centre

Visitors can build a roller coaster at the Ontario Science Centre in Canada. In doing so, they learn about the scientific **principles** of energy, force, and **friction**.

National Air and Space Museum

People visiting the National Air and Space Museum in Washington, D.C., can experience space travel with a virtual ride into space. Visitors can blast off in a rocket, go for a spacewalk, or take a tour of the galaxy.

More than **1 million people visit the Ontario Science Centre** every year.

The Carnegie Museum's **dinosaur fossils** are estimated to be **worth more than $200 million**.

The West of the Pecos Museum has **more than 50 rooms** of **exhibits**.

Tour guides try to tailor their talks to the group they are leading. They may introduce materials to encourage discussion around certain works or topics.

Things to Do in a Museum

Taking a tour is a great way to see a museum. Some museums hold tours every day. During a tour, a museum worker walks through the galleries with visitors. He or she tells them more about the objects on display.

Museums plan a variety of special events throughout the year. People can hear experts give talks about art, science, or history. They can visit special exhibits that are only at the museum for a short time. Some museums even hold sleepovers.

The Field Museum, in Chicago, Illinois, has a program called "Dozin' with the Dinos." It allows guests to spend a night in its Hall of Dinosaurs.

Museum Manners

Visiting a museum is a special experience. It is important that everyone is allowed to enjoy their time in the facility. There are many ways to show respect for a museum and its visitors.

6 Simple Rules

1. Do not touch any of the objects on display unless a museum worker gives you permission.
2. Speak softly and use an "indoor" voice.
3. Walk through the galleries. Do not run or jump.
4. Do not take any food or drink into the galleries.
5. Ask a museum worker if it is all right to take pictures of the works on display.
6. Ask your guide questions about the objects on display, and be a good listener.

Museum guides spend considerable time preparing for a class visit. Listening closely to them when they are speaking shows respect for the work they have done to plan the tour.

A History of Museums

The world's first museum was established more than 2,500 years ago. Since then, museums have come to be places where people honor and pay tribute to the past.

1500s

Collectors open private museums across Europe.

6th Century BC

Princess Ennigaldi of **Babylon** develops the world's first known museum.

1471 AD

The Capitoline Museum is established in Rome, Italy. It is often considered to be the world's first modern museum.

Oxford University opens the Ashmolean Museum. It is the first museum to open to the general public.

The Musée du Louvre opens its first **satellite** museum in the French town of Lens. It has since opened another satellite in Abu Dhabi.

1683

1899

2012

2019

The Brooklyn Children's Museum is founded in New York. It is the world's first museum for children.

More than 7 million people visit New York's Metropolitan Museum of Art, making it the most visited museum in the United States.

Who Works in a Museum?

A museum requires the skills of many people. Some work behind the scenes. Others work directly with the public.

Conservator

The conservator keeps a museum's collection in good condition. He or she repairs parts that are damaged. The conservator also makes sure that the museum displays its collections in a safe way.

Exhibit Designer

The exhibit designer decides how a gallery should look. He or she plans the **layout** of a room and organizes the objects on display. This person may even choose the color of paint to use on the walls.

Curator

Curators are the people who plan the museum's exhibits. They make sure that the items on display fit the **theme** of the exhibit. Curators also search for new items to add to the museum's collection.

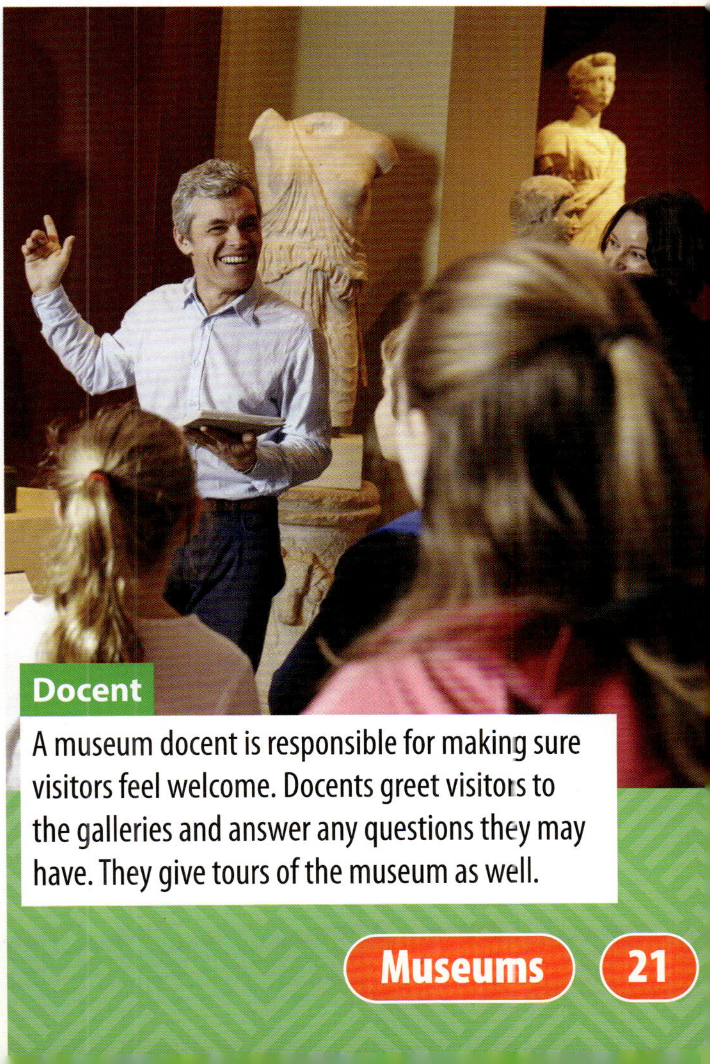

Docent

A museum docent is responsible for making sure visitors feel welcome. Docents greet visitors to the galleries and answer any questions they may have. They give tours of the museum as well.

10 Questions to Test Your Knowledge

1. How many museums does the United States have?
2. What kind of museum is likely to have dinosaur fossils?
3. Where is a virtual museum found?
4. What is the name of the world's largest art museum?

5. What are the rooms in a museum called?
6. Which country is home to the Ontario Science Centre?
7. Which Chicago museum holds an event called "Dozin' with the Dinos"?

8. Which type of voice should be used in a museum?
9. Who developed the world's first known museum?
10. Which worker keeps a museum's collection in good condition?

ANSWERS: 1. More than 35,000 **2.** Natural history museum **3.** Online **4.** Musée du Louvre **5.** Galleries **6.** Canada **7.** The Field Museum **8.** An "indoor" voice **9.** Princess Ennigaldi of Babylon **10.** Conservator

Key Words

artifacts: tools, weapons, or other objects made by people in the past

Babylon: an ancient kingdom in what is now Iraq

collections: objects that have been gathered together for study or show

fossils: the hardened remains of animals or plants that lived long ago

friction: the rubbing of one object against another

habitat: the natural home or environment of an animal, plant, or other organism

layout: the way in which the parts of something are arranged

pioneers: people who are among the first to explore and settle a region

principles: general truths on which theories can be based

satellite: a branch of a larger organization that is located away from the main part

sculptures: figures or designs made by carving wood, stone, or other materials

theme: the main subject or idea of something

Index

Get the best of both worlds.

AV2 bridges the gap between print and digital.

The expandable resources toolbar enables quick access to content including **videos**, **audio**, **activities**, **weblinks**, **slideshows**, **quizzes**, and **key words**.

Animated videos make static images come alive.

Resource icons on each page help readers to further **explore key concepts**.

Published by AV2
14 Penn Plaza 9th Floor
New York, NY 10122
Website: www.av2books.com

Library of Congress Cataloging-in-Publication Data
Names: Kissock, Heather, author.
Title: Museums / Heather Kissock.
Description: New York, NY : AV2, [2021] | Series: Field trips | Includes index. | Audience: Grades 4-6 |
Identifiers: LCCN 2020010941 (print) | LCCN 2020010942 (ebook) | ISBN 9781791121594 (library binding) | ISBN 9781791121600 (paperback) | ISBN 9781791121617 | ISBN 9781791121624
Subjects: LCSH: Museums--Juvenile literature. | School field trips--Juvenile literature.
Classification: LCC AM7 .K57 2021 (print) | LCC AM7 (ebook) | DDC 069--dc23
LC record available at https://lccn.loc.gov/2020010941
LC ebook record available at https://lccn.loc.gov/2020010942LC ebook record available at https://lccn.loc.gov/2019050480

Printed in Guangzhou, China
1 2 3 4 5 6 7 8 9 0 24 23 22 21 20

052020
101119

Editor: Heather Kissock
Designer: Terry Paulhus

AV2 acknowledges Getty Images, Alamy, iStock, Shutterstock, Wikimedia Commons, and Ontario Science Centre as its primary image suppliers for this title.